Everyday English

Book 2
Second Edition

Everyday English

Book 2
Second Edition

Barbara Zaffran
Staff Development Specialist in
ESL and Native Languages
New York City

David Krulik
Former Director
Secondary-School ESL Programs
New York City

428.2
Z17e
1992
Vol. 2

National Textbook Company
a division of *NTC Publishing Group* • Lincolnwood, Illinois USA

11/97

*To Alain, with love
and remembrance*

Cover Photo Credits: ©Brent Jones (top left); R. Krubner/H. Armstrong Roberts (top right, bottom right); J. Swider/H. Armstrong Roberts (bottom left)

1997 Printing

Published by National Textbook Company, a division of NTC Publishing Group.
©1991 by NTC Publishing Group, 4255 West Touhy Avenue,
Lincolnwood (Chicago), Illinois 60646-1975 U.S.A.
Manufactured in the United States of America.

6 7 8 9 VP 9 8 7

Contents

Unit 1 Time

Lesson 1   Parts of a Day

Exercise 1   Answer these questions in complete sentences.

1. What time do you get up? _____

2. What time do you go to school? _____

3. What time do you go to work? _____

4. What time do you eat lunch? _____

5. What time do you go to sleep? _____

Exercise 2   Study these sentences and pictures with your teacher.

1. The numbers 1–12 are on a clock's <u>face</u>.

2. The <u>minute hand</u> (long hand) points to the minutes.

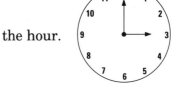

3. The <u>hour hand</u> (short hand) points to the hour.

4. The <u>second hand</u> moves fastest. It tells the seconds.

5. An <u>alarm clock</u> rings to wake us up in the morning.

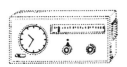

6. A <u>clock radio</u> plays music to wake us up.

Exercise 3   Write the correct words on the lines below the pictures.

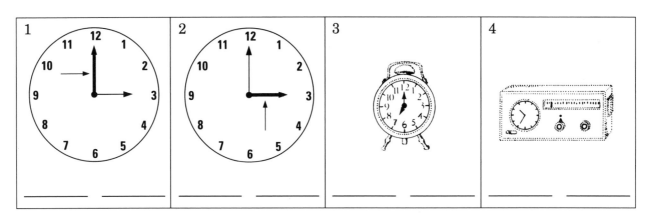

1	2	3	4
_____	_____	_____ _____	_____ _____

Exercise 4   When the minute hand is on the 12 and the hour hand is on the 1, we say that it is one **o'clock**.

a. Complete the faces of these clocks by writing the numerals 1–12 in the correct places.

b. Now draw hands on the clocks to show (1) eleven o'clock, (2) four o'clock, (3) eight o'clock, (4) three o'clock, and (5) seven o'clock.

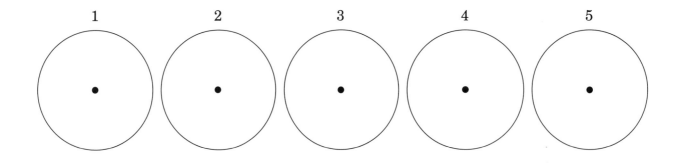

1   2   3   4   5

c. Now write each of the above times, using numerals.

1. _____   4. _____

2. _____   5. _____

3. _____

d. Indicate that clocks 1, 3, and 5 show morning hours. Indicate that clocks 2 and 4 show afternoon hours.

1. _____   4. _____

2. _____   5. _____

3. _____

Lesson 2 Telling Time: Hours and Half Hours

Exercise 1   What time is it?

Write each time in words and then in numerals.

   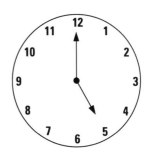

_____   _____   _____   _____

_____   _____   _____   _____

Exercise 2   Draw hands on each clock to show the correct time.

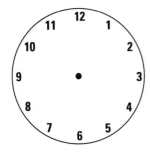 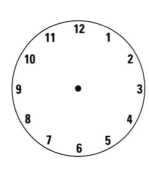 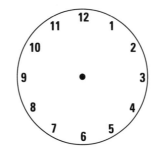 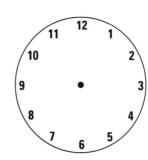

five o'clock   nine o'clock   four o'clock   three o'clock

Exercise 3   Read each sentence and fill in the blank with the correct time of the day.

morning   evening   afternoon   night

1. I get up in the _____ .

2. I eat lunch in the _____ .

3. I eat dinner in the _____ .

4. I sleep at _____ .

5. I do my homework in the _____ .

Exercise 4   Study these paragraphs with your teacher.

Midnight and **noon** are two special times. **Midnight** is twelve o'clock at night. Most people are asleep at midnight. **Noon** is twelve o'clock in the daytime. Many people eat lunch at noon.

These are the only times that have special names. With all other times, we can use the abbreviations A.M. and P.M. to show what time of day or night we mean.

- A.M. is used with times in the morning (between midnight and noon).

- P.M. is used with times in the afternoon, in the evening, and at night (between noon and midnight).

Examples:

1. I get up at 7:00 A.M.
2. I do my homework at 7:00 P.M.

Exercise 5   Circle the best answer for each question.

1. When do you eat breakfast?

   a. 7:00 A.M.   b. 7:00 P.M.

2. When are you asleep?

   a. noon   b. midnight

3. When do you eat dinner?

   a. 6:00 A.M.   b. 6:00 P.M.

4. When do you eat lunch?

    a. noon   b. midnight

5. When do you get home from school?

    a. 4:00 A.M.   b. 4:00 P.M.

Exercise 6   Write each time in words.

1. 7:00 A.M. _____

2. 8:00 P.M. _____

3. 9:00 P.M. _____

4. 4:00 A.M. _____

5. 11:00 A.M. _____

Exercise 7   When the hour hand is on the 1 and the minute hand is on the six, we say it is **_one thirty_**.

Draw hands on these clocks to show the correct times.

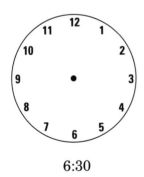   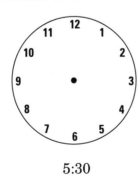   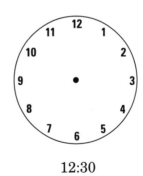   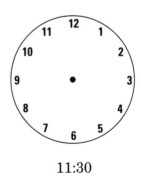

    6:30   5:30   12:30   11:30

Exercise 8   Write each time in words

1. 1:30 _____   6. 3:00 _____

2. 4:30 _____   7. 7:30 _____

3. 5:00 _____   8. 9:00 _____

4. 10:00 _____   9. 2:30 _____

5. 8:30 _____   10. 6:30 _____

Exercise 9   When we see this time — 1:30 — we say "one thirty." We can also say "half past one." **Half past one** and **one thirty** are two different ways to say the same thing — 1:30. Write these times in two different ways.

1. 10:30 _____   _____

2. 7:30 _____   _____

3. 2:30 _____   _____

4. 5:30 _____   _____

5. 11:30 _____   _____

Exercise 10   What time is it? Write a sentence for each clock.

Example: It's 2:30.

_____ _____ _____ _____ _____

Lesson 3   **Reading and Writing Time in Numerals**

Exercise 1   Look at the time on this clock. There are two different ways to say this time: **one fifteen** or a **quarter after one**. In numerals, we write **1:15**.

Now look at these clocks and fill in the blanks to complete the times.

1. 1. one _____   _____ one

2. 2. two _____   _____ two

3. 3. three _____   _____ three

4. 4. nine _____   _____ nine

5. 5. eleven _____   _____ eleven

Everyday English, Book Two

Exercise 2

Look at the time on this clock.
There are two different ways to say this time:
one forty-five or **a quarter to two**.
In numerals, we write **1:45**.

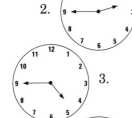 1.

Now look at these clocks and fill in the blanks to complete the times.

1. one _____   _____ two

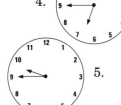 2.

2. two _____   _____ three

 3.

3. four _____   _____ five

4. six _____   _____ seven

5. nine _____   _____ ten

Exercise 3

What time is it? Write a sentence for each clock.

Example: It's 5:45.

         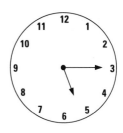

_____   _____   _____   _____   _____

Exercise 4

Write each time in words.

1. 1:00 _____   6. 11:15 _____

2. 3:30 _____   7. 7:30 _____

3. 6:45 _____   8. 12:30 _____

4. 8:00 _____   9. 12:45 _____

5. 9:15 _____   10. 9:00 _____

Exercise 5 Write each time in three different ways. One way must be in numerals.

_____

_____

_____

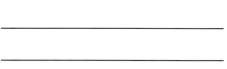

_____

_____

_____

_____

_____

_____

_____

_____

_____

_____

Exercise 6 Write each time in numerals.

1. seven forty-five   _____

2. a quarter to eight   _____

3. eight fifteen   _____

4. a quarter after eight   _____

5. nine o'clock   _____

6. four fifteen   _____

7. a quarter after four _____

8. a quarter to four _____

9. twelve thirty _____

10. half past twelve _____

Lesson **4**   **Telling Time: Minutes**

Exercise 1   Study this clock with your teacher.

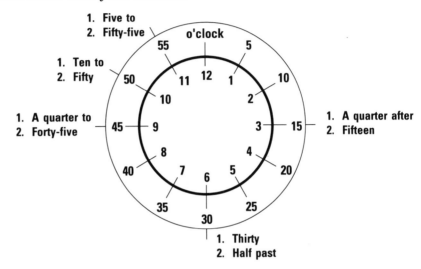

Exercise 2   Use numerals to write the correct time below each clock.

a. o'clock

_____   _____   _____   _____   _____

b. half past

_____   _____   _____   _____   _____

c. a quarter after

 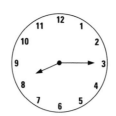   

_____ _____ _____ _____ _____

d. a quarter to

    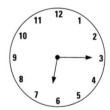

_____ _____ _____ _____ _____

e. various times

    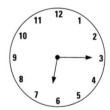

_____ _____ _____ _____ _____

Lesson 5 Talking about Periods of Time

Exercise 1 Study these sentences.

1. There are sixty minutes in an hour.

2. If it is seven fifty-five, it is five to eight.

3. When the minute hand is between the six and the twelve, we indicate the time by saying, for example, that it is "twenty **to** seven."

Exercise 2 Complete these sentences.

1. If it is six thirty-five, it is twenty-five to seven.

2. If it is seven fifty, it is _____ .

3. If it is ten fifty-seven, it is _____ .

4. If it is four forty, it is _____ .

5. If it is nine fifty-five, it is _____ .

6. If it is eight forty-five, it is _____ .

Exercise 3   What time is it? Write a sentence for each clock.

Example: It's 8:35.

 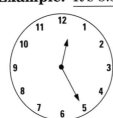   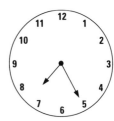

_____   _____   _____   _____   _____

Exercise 4   Write each time in words.

1. 1:40 _____   6. 2:55 _____

2. 4:35 _____   7. 1:10 _____

3. 7:20 _____   8. 5:05 _____

4. 9:25 _____   9. 3:15 _____

5. 8:50 _____   10. 11:45 _____

Exercise 5   Write each time in three different ways. (One way must be in numerals.)

_____   _____

_____   _____

_____   _____

_____

_____

_____

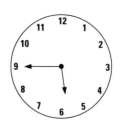

_____

_____

_____

_____

_____

_____

Exercise 6 Write these times in numerals.

1. seven fifty _____

6. five to eleven _____

2. eight forty-five _____

7. twenty to four _____

3. a quarter to nine _____

8. twenty after four _____

4. five thirty _____

9. a quarter after one _____

5. ten to six _____

10. twenty-five to three _____

Exercise 7 Draw the correct time on each clock face.

a. It's eight o'clock.

b. It's twenty-five to four.

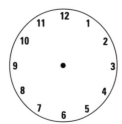

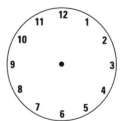

c. It's a quarter after seven.

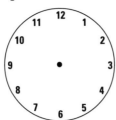

d. It's two thirty.

e. It's a quarter to five.

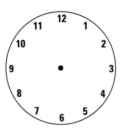

f. It's ten after six.

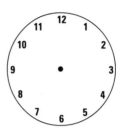

Exercise 8   Answer these questions in complete sentences.

1. What time do you wake up in the morning?

   _____

2. What time do you eat breakfast?

   _____

3. What time do you eat lunch?

   _____

4. What time do you eat dinner?

   _____

5. What time do you go to bed?

   _____

Lesson **6**   Reading and Writing the Time in Words

Exercise 1   Write each time in words.

_____   _____

_____   _____

Exercise 2   Write the correct words in the blanks.

What's this?   What's this?

   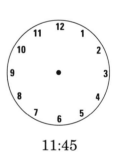

It's an _____ _____ .   It's a _____ .

Exercise 3   Draw hands on these clock faces to show the correct times.

      8:45   3:00   7:30   4:15   11:45

Now draw hands on these clock faces and write each time in numerals.

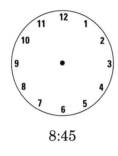   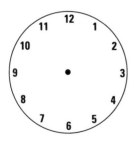   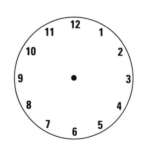   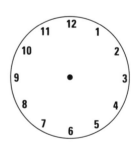

five after six   ten to twelve   nine forty-five   half past ten

     6:05

_____   _____   _____   _____

Exercise 4 Write each time in three different ways. (One way must be in numerals.)

_____

_____

_____

_____

_____

_____

_____

_____

_____

_____

_____

_____

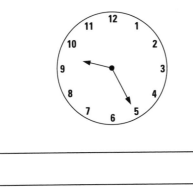

_____

_____

_____

Exercise 5 Write each time in words.

1. 9:00 A.M. _____

2. 7:45 A.M. _____

3. 9:50 P.M. _____

4. 5:55 A.M. _____

5. 2:15 P.M. _____

Exercise 6   What time is it? Write a sentence for each clock.

Example: It's 6:15.

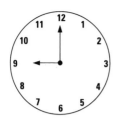    

_____   _____   _____   _____   _____

Exercise 7   Write each time in words.

1. 1:50 _____   6. 5:05 _____

2. 4:45 _____   7. 3:15 _____

3. 8:25 _____   8. 2:55 _____

4. 7:50 _____   9. 7:20 _____

5. 8:10 _____   10. 1:30 _____

Exercise 8   Write each time in numerals.

1. eight forty-five _____

2. a quarter to seven _____

3. five fifty _____

4. ten to six _____

5. a quarter to two _____

Exercise 9   Circle the correct answer to complete each sentence.

1. I get up in the _____ .

   a. morning   b. evening   c. afternoon

2. I eat lunch at _____ .

   a. midnight   b. night   c. noon

3. I do my homework in the _____ .

   a. morning   b. evening   c. afternoon

4. I eat breakfast in the in the _____ .

    a. morning   b. evening   c. night

5. I am asleep at _____ .

    a. noon   b. afternoon   c. midnight

Exercise 10   Complete the crossword puzzle. Write each time in numerals. Do not use colons (:).

Across

1 A quarter to two.

3 Five to seven.

6 Ten after three.

7 Half past ten.

8 Twenty-five after six.

13 Two minutes after nine.

14 Twenty-two minutes to two.

16 Fifteen minutes to six.

17 Four o'clock.

18 Midnight.

Down

1 Four minutes to two.

2 Twenty-five to six.

3 Five after six.

4 A quarter after five.

5 Five thirty-five.

9 Twenty-one minutes to three.

10 Ten to one.

11 Ten to twelve.

12 Ten o'clock.

15 Twenty to nine.

Unit 2 The Family

Lesson 7   Members of a Family

Exercise 1   Study this picture and read the sentences below.

     a. This is Mary Abeyto. She is a **mother**.

     b. This is Charles Abeyto. He's a **father**.

     c. This is Annie Abeyto. She's a **child**.

     d. This is Johnny Abeyto. He's a **child**, too.

        Annie and Johnny are **children**.

     e. This is Jimmy Abeyto. He is a little child. He's a **baby**.

Exercise 2   Answer these questions in complete sentences.

     1. Who is Mary Abeyto? _____

     2. Who is Charles Abeyto? _____

     3. Who is Annie? _____

     4. Who is Johnny? _____

     5. Who is Jimmy? _____

Exercise 3   Study these sentences with your teacher.

1. Johnny is Annie and Jimmy's **brother**.
2. Annie is Johnny and Jimmy's **sister**.
3. Annie, Johnny, and Jimmy are **children**.
4. Mr. and Mrs. Abeyto are **parents**.
5. Mary is Charles's **wife**.
6. Charles is Mary's **husband**.
7. Johnny and Jimmy are Mr. and Mrs. Abeyto's **sons**.
8. Annie is Mr. and Mrs. Abeyto's **daughter**.

Exercise 4   Complete the sentences.

1. Annie's mother is _____ .

2. Charles and Mary's daughter is _____ .

3. The children's parents are _____ .

4. Mrs. Abeyto's husband is _____ .

5. Charles's wife is _____ .

6. Mary and Charles are the _____ of
   Annie, Johnny, and Jimmy.

7. Jimmy is the _____ .

8. Annie, Johnny, and Jimmy are _____ .

9. Annie's father is _____ .

10. Charles and Mary's sons are _____ .

Exercise 5   Unscramble these words.

1. r h r o e b t _____
2. t a e n p r _____
3. h l r n i c d e _____
4. a h r f e t _____
5. o h r e t m _____

6. t i e s s r _____
7. l h d c i _____
8. o n s _____
9. g a t r d u h e _____
10. y b b a _____

Exercise 6   Look at these pictures of families and complete the sentences.

a. This is a woman.

   She is the _____ of this child.

   She is her husband's _____ .

b. This is a man.

   He is the _____ of these children.

   He is his wife's _____ .

   He and his wife are the children's _____ .

c. This is a boy.

   He is his mother's _____ .

   He is his sister's _____ .

d. This is a girl.

   She is her father's _____ .

   She is her brother's _____ .

   She and her brother are their father's _____ .

Lesson **8**   A Family Tree

Exercise 1   Study this family tree for the Abeyto family.

Note: The symbol = means **married to**, and the symbol | means **children of**.

 =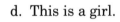

Charles Abeyto   Mary Abeyto

Annie Abeyto   Johnny Abeyto   Jimmy Abeyto

Everyday English, Book Two

Exercise 2   Answer these questions in complete sentences.

1. What is Annie's mother's name? _____

_____

2. What is Jimmy's father's name? _____

_____

3. What are Johnny's parents' names? _____

_____

4. What is Johnny's sister's name? _____

_____

5. What is Jimmy's brother's name? _____

_____

6. What is Charles's daughter's name? _____

_____

7. What is Charles's wife's name? _____

_____

8. What is Mary's husband's name? _____

_____

9. What is the baby's name? _____

_____

10. What are Mary's sons' names? _____

_____

Exercise 3   Study these sentences with your teacher.

1. Mr. and Mrs. Abeyto's parents are the **grandparents** of Annie, Johnny, and Jimmy.
2. Mr. and Mrs. Abeyto's fathers are Annie, Johnny, and Jimmy's **grandfathers**.
3. Mr. and Mrs. Abeyto's mothers are Annie, Johnny, and Jimmy's **grandmothers**.
4. Annie, Johnny, and Jimmy call them **Grandpa** and **Grandma**.
5. Annie, Johnny, and Jimmy are the **grandchildren**.
6. Johnny and Jimmy are the **grandsons**.
7. Annie is the **granddaughter**.

Exercise 4   Complete these sentences with words from the list below.

sisters	granddaughter	grandchildren	grandfather
brothers	grandson	grandmother	grandparents

1. Your parents' parents are your _____ .

2. Your parents' children are your grandparents' _____ .

3. Your brother is your grandparents' _____ .

4. Your sister is your grandparents' _____ .

5. Your mother's father is your _____ .

6. Your father's father is your _____ .

7. Your mother's mother is your _____ .

8. Your father's mother is your _____ .

9. Johnny and Jimmy are _____ .

10. Annie is their _____ .

Exercise 5   Study these sentences with your teacher.

1. Mr. and Mrs. Abeyto's sisters are the children's **aunts**.
2. Mr. and Mrs. Abeyto's brothers are the children's **uncles**.
3. Johnny is the **nephew** of Mr. and Mr. Abeyto's brothers and sisters.
4. Annie is the **niece** of Mr. and Mrs. Abeyto's brothers and sisters.
5. Mr. and Mrs. Abeyto's nephews and nieces are Annie, Johnny, and Jimmy's **cousins**.

Exercise 6   Look in column B to find what we call each person described in column A. Write the correct letters on the lines.

A	**B**
____ 1. my mother's sister	a. my nephew
____ 2. my father's mother	b. my aunt
____ 3. my sister's son	c. my uncle
____ 4. my mother's father	d. his niece
____ 5. my mother's son	e. my cousins
____ 6. my aunt's husband	f. my grandpa
____ 7. my uncle's children	g. my brother
____ 8. my father's sister's daughter	h. my grandmother

Exercise 7   Complete the Abeyto family tree. Make up names for the children's grandparents, aunt, uncle, and cousin.

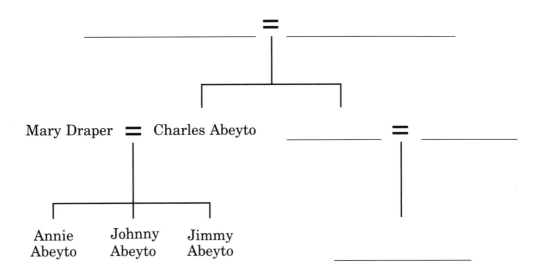

Exercise 8   Circle the best answer for each question.

1. My sister is my father's _____ .

   a. mother   b. daughter   c. son

2. My brother's daughter is my _____ .

   a. nephew   b. sister   c. niece

3. My mother's sister is my _____ .

   a. grandmother   b. aunt   c. uncle

4. My father's wife is my _____ .

   a. mother   b. grandmother   c. aunt

5. My niece is my mother's _____ .

   a. grandchild   b. nephew   c. daughter

Exercise 1   Answer these questions about your family in complete sentences.

   1. Who's the oldest? _____

   _____

   2. Who's the youngest? _____

   _____

   3. Who's the strongest? _____

   _____

   4. Who's the tallest? _____

   _____

   5. Who's the shortest? _____

   _____

   6. Who's the funniest? _____

   _____

   7. Who's the quietest? _____

   _____

   8. Who's the smartest? _____

   _____

   9. Who lives in the same city as you do? _____

   _____

   _____

   10. Who lives in another city, another state, or another country?

   _____

   _____

Exercise 2   Read this dialogue.

   Alan: Hi, Barbara.

   Barbara: Hi, Alan.

Everyday English, Book Two

Alan:	Where's your sister? I want to speak to her.
Barbara:	She's at my cousin's house. You know, the house of my father's sister's child.
Alan:	You just gave me an idea. Let's see how good we are at family relationships. I'll start a sentence, and you'll finish it. Your cousin is your mother's . . .
Barbara:	nephew or niece. Now it's my turn. You are your mother's . . .
Alan:	son. Your mother's mother is your . . .
Barbara:	grandmother. Your father's father is your . . .
Alan:	grandfather. And your father's daughter is your . . .
Barbara:	sister. Hey, this is fun! Let's go on. Your father's mother is your . . .
Alan:	grandmother. I am my sister's . . .
Barbara:	brother. Your father is your mother's . . .
Alan:	husband. Your mother is your father's . . .
Barbara:	wife. The smallest child in the family is the . . .
Alan:	baby. Your aunt's husband is your . . .
Barbara:	uncle. I'm sorry, but I have to leave now. I'm going to be late for a meeting.
Alan:	O.K. Please tell your mother's daughter, your aunt's niece, and your grandmother's granddaughter that I want to speak to her.
Barbara:	O.K. I will. See you later.
Alan:	Bye.

Exercise 3   Answer these questions in complete sentences.

Example: Who is your aunt's husband? <u>He is my uncle.</u>

1. Who is your aunt's daughter?_____

2. Who is your mother's son? _____

3. Who is your father's wife? _____

4. Who is your cousin's father? _____

5. Who is your mother's mother? _____

6. Who is your sister's son? _____

7. Who is your mother's husband? _____

8. Who is your uncle's wife? _____

9. Who is your grandmother's child? _____

10. Who is your mother's sister's daughter? _____

Exercise 4   Make your own family tree. Include your grandparents, parents, brothers and sisters, aunts, uncles, and cousins. Look at the Abeyto family tree if you need help. Remember that the symbol = means **married to** and the symbol │ means **children of**.

Exercise 5   Study these relationships with your teacher.

1. Your **spouse** is your husband or wife.
2. When you marry, your spouse's mother, father, sisters, and brothers become your **in-laws**. Thet means that, by law, they are your relatives.
3. Your **father-in-law** is your spouse's father.
4. Your **mother-in-law** is your spouse's mother.
5. Your **sister-in-law** is your spouse's sister.
6. Your **brother-in-law** is your spouse's brother.
7. If your mother remarries, her new husband is your **stepfather**.
8. If your father remarries, his new wife is your **stepmother**.
9. Your stepfather and stepmother are your **stepparents**.
10. Their children are your **stepsisters** and **stepbrothers**.
11. You are your stepparents' **stepchild** (a **stepdaughter** or **stepson**).

Exercise 6   Look in column B to find what we call each person described in column A. Write the correct letters on the lines.

A	B
____ 1. my wife's sister	a. my father-in-law
____ 2. my brother's daughter	b. my aunt
____ 3. my husband's father	c. my sister-in-law
____ 4. my father's mother	d. my niece
____ 5. my cousin's mother	e. my grandmother

Lesson 10 Review of Family Members and Relationships

Exercise 1   Read the sentences and write **True** or **False** on the line next to each one.

1. My uncle's wife is my aunt. _____
2. My mother's daughter is my son. _____
3. My aunt's children are my cousins. _____
4. My grandma and grandpa are my father's or mother's parents. _____
5. My uncle is my father's nephew. _____

Exercise 2   Complete the sentences.

1. Your father's brother is your _____ .

2. Your husband's mother is your _____ .

3. Your father's sister is your _____ .

4. Your brother's daughter is your _____ .

5. Your brother's wife is your _____ .

6. Your father's mother is your _____ .

7. Your cousin's sister is your _____ .

8. Your aunt's daughter is your _____ .

9. Your aunt's husband is your _____ .

10. Your wife's brother is your _____ .

11. Your stepfather's daughter is your _____ .

12. Your husband's father is your _____ .

Exercise 3

aunt
baby
boy
brother
child
cousin
daughter
father
girl
grandfather
grandmother
house
husband
in-laws
kid
mother
nephew
niece
parents
sister
son
spouse
tree
uncle
wife

Find and circle the hidden words. Look across, down, diagonally, forward, and backward. Then find the eleven letters you do not use. Unscramble them and they will tell you where to look to find out about your family history. Write the mystery words below the puzzle.

M	S	D	A	U	G	H	T	E	R	F	S
G	O	A	M	N	H	O	U	S	E	D	P
R	N	T	I	C	C	O	U	S	I	N	O
A	R	P	H	L	C	H	I	L	D	A	U
N	E	A	B	E	L	E	R	Y	S	B	S
D	H	R	A	T	R	E	C	W	R	S	E
M	T	E	B	E	T	Y	A	E	G	U	F
O	O	N	Y	S	O	L	E	I	I	H	A
T	R	T	I	B	N	E	R	A	U	N	T
H	B	S	S	I	R	L	E	K	I	D	H
E	F	I	W	T	W	E	H	P	E	N	E
R	G	R	A	N	D	F	A	T	H	E	R

Mystery Words: F _ _ _ _ _   T _ _ _ _

Exercise 4   Unscramble the words at the left. Write one letter in each box at the right. Then unscramble the letters in th circles to spell out the mystery word.

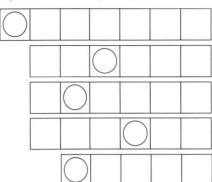

1. s a b u n h d

2. r i t e s s

3. o h r m t e

4. p a n t e r

5. l u n c e

Mystery Word: __ __ __ __ __

Exercise 5   Complete the crossword puzzle.

Across

1 My father's father is my _____ .

4 My brother's wife is my sister- _____ .

6 My brother is my mother's _____ .

7 My sister's son is my _____ .

10 My sister's daughter is my _____ .

13 My sister is my father's _____ .

14 A short name for mother is _____ .

16 My father is my mother's _____ .

20 My brother is a baby. _____ is a boy.

21 My aunt's children are my _____ .

23 I put the rice in a _____ .

24 We climbed to the top of the _____ .

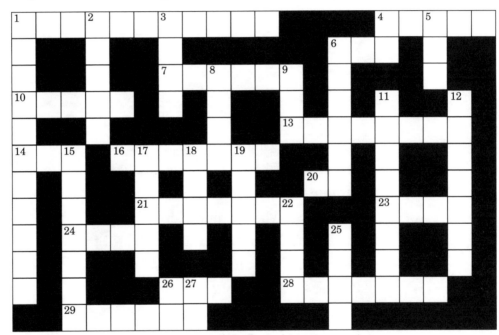

26 A young man is a _____ .

28 My mother and father are my _____ .

29 My parents' daughter is my _____ .

Down

1 My father's mother is my _____ .

2 My brother's daughter is my _____ .

3 My father's sister is my _____ .

4 My husband's father is my father- _____-law.

5 My brother's wife is my sister-in-_____ .

6 A wife is her husband's _____ .

8 A short name for father is _____ .

9 A synonym for **married** is _____ .

11 The plural for child is _____ .

12 My father's son is my _____ .

15 My _____ sister is my aunt.

17 My aunt's husband is my _____ .

18 A traditional color for baby clothes is _____ .

19 Children often make a lot of _____ .

22 Wash your hands with _____ .

25 My niece is a baby _____ .

26 I want to _____ a good son.

27 I want another sister _____ brother.

Unit 3 School

Lesson 11 The First Day

Exercise 1   Read the dialogue. You can change the underlined words so that the dialogue will tell about you and your teacher.

Teacher:	My name is <u>Mrs. Book</u>. What's your name.
Student:	My name is <u>Joe</u>.
Teacher:	What country are you from?
Student:	I come from <u>Switzerland</u>.
Teacher:	How did you come here?
Student:	I came by <u>plane</u>.
Teacher:	Where do you live now?
Student:	I live in the United States, in <u>Chicago</u>.
Teacher:	What is your address?
Student:	My address is <u>1501 Maple Street</u>.
Teacher:	What is your telephone number?
Student:	My telephone number is <u>555–4284</u>.
Teacher:	Where do you go to school?
Student:	I go to school at <u>Shorefront High</u>.
Teacher:	It was nice meeting you. See you tomorrow.
Student:	So long. Nice meeting you, too.

Exercise 2   Answer the questions in complete sentences.

1. What's your name?_____

_____

2. What's your teacher's name? _____

_____

3. What country are you from?_____

_____

4. How did you come to the United States? _____

_____

5. In what city do you live? _____

_____

6. In what state do you live? _____

_____

7. What is your address? _____

_____

8. What is your telephone number? _____

_____

9. Where do you go to school? _____

_____

10. What grade are you in? _____

_____

Exercise 3   Write a question for each answer. Remember to put a question mark (?) at the end of each question.

1. My name is Lucy. _____

2. I'm from Cuba. _____

3. I live in the United States now. _____

_____

4. I live in Miami. _____

5. My address is 1978 York Street. _____

6. I go to Central High School. _____

_____

7. My teacher's name is Mr. Hawthorne. _____

_____

8. I'm in the ninth grade. _____

Lesson 12 Things in the Classroom

Exercise 1   Make a list of objects in your classroom.

_____   _____

_____   _____

_____   _____

_____   _____

_____   _____

_____   _____

_____   _____

_____   _____

_____   _____

_____   _____

_____   _____

_____   _____

Exercise 2   Unscramble the words and then match them to the pictures. Write the letter of the correct picture on the line next to each word.

____ 1. s e d k   _____   ____ 11. l e n p i c   _____

____ 2. o d o r   _____   ____ 12. y n a r c o s   _____

____ 3. e n p   _____   ____ 13. l o s t e c   _____

____ 4. ratsh nac   _____   ____ 14. liifgn batince   _____

____ 5. s a e r r e   _____   ____ 15. l c a k h   _____

____ 6. a r i c h   _____   ____ 16. b a l e t   _____

____ 7. toca hokos   _____   ____ 17. g t i h l s   _____

____ 8. d i o n w w   _____   ____ 18. k o o b   _____

____ 9. t o n e b o k o   _____   ____ 19. t i u e p c r s   _____

____ 10. h a l c k d r o a b _____   ____ 20. l u e r r   _____

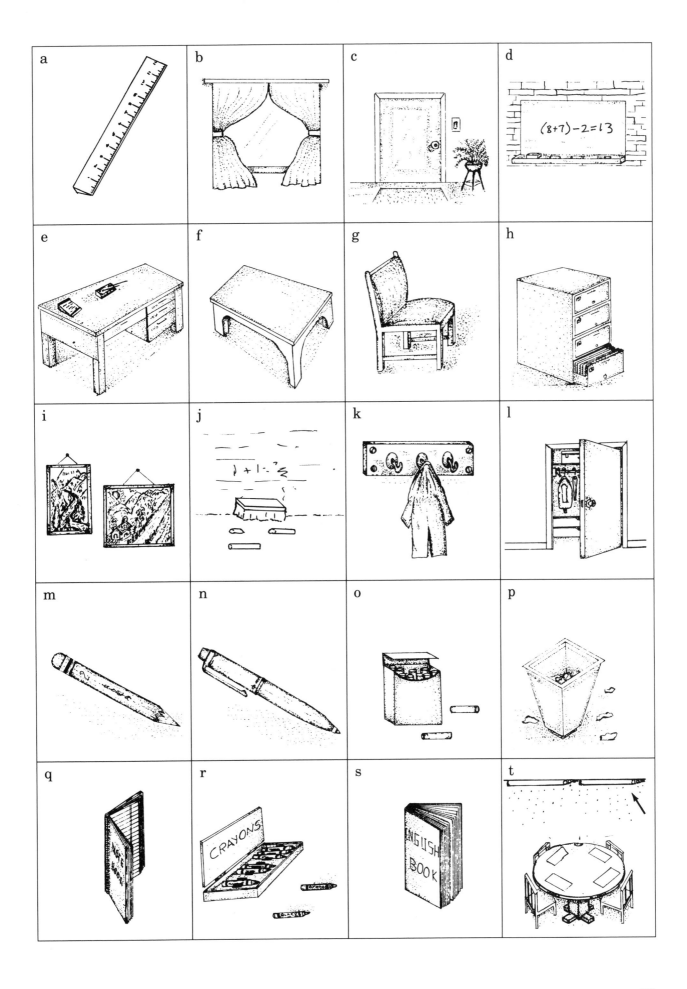

Exercise 3   Complete each sentence with a word from exercise 2. Use any word that makes sense.

1. I sit on a _____ .

2. We clean the chalkboard with an _____ .

3. I put my _____ on the desk.

4. We write with a _____ or a _____ .

5. We read a _____ .

6. We color with _____ .

7. We throw garbage in the _____ .

8. We hang our coats on _____ .

9. We open the _____ when it's hot.

10. We turn on the _____ when it's dark.

Lesson **13** People and Places in Our School

Exercise 1   Read these sentences with your teacher.

1. We eat in the cafeteria.
2. We find books in the library.
3. We get help with our problems from the guidance counselor.
4. If we feel sick, we visit the nurse or doctor.
5. We get paint in the art room.
6. We hear a concert in the auditorium.
7. We watch a basketball game in the gym.
8. We speak to the principal in the main office.
9. We play soccer or football on the athletic field.
10. We go to the bathroom and wash our hands in the restroom.

Exercise 2   Complete the sentences.

1. We eat in the _____ .

2. We _____ in the library.

3. We _____ from the guidance counselor.

4. If we feel sick, we _____ .

5. We get paint in the _____ .

Everyday English, Book Two

6. We hear a concert in the _____ .

7. We _____ in the gym.

8. We speak to the _____ in the main office.

9. We play soccer or football on the _____ .

10. We go to the bathroom and wash our hands in the _____ .

Exercise 3   Answer these questions in complete sentences.

1. Where do we play soccer? _____

_____

2. Where do we hear a concert? _____

_____

3. Where do we eat? _____

_____

4. Who can help us with a problem? _____

_____

5. Where do we wash our hands? _____

_____

6. Where do we get paint? _____

_____

7. Where do we check out books? _____

_____

8. Where do we play basketball? _____

_____

9. Where do we go if we feel sick? _____

_____

10. Where do we go to speak to the principal? _____

_____

Exercise 4 Find the room numbers in your school for these services. Write the correct room numbers in the blanks. If your school doesn't have a service, write **no** in the blank. If the service has no room number, write **yes** in the blank.

1. nurse's office _____
2. gym _____
3. doctor's office _____
4. library _____
5. restroom _____

6. auditorium _____
7. guidance counselor's office _____
8. principal's office _____
9. cafeteria _____
10. art room _____

Make a list of other important room numbers you need to know.

_____

_____

_____

Exercise 5 Complete the dialogue with vocabulary words from this unit.

Teacher: Good morning, class. Please hang your coats on the _____ and sit down. Then open to page 35 in your _____ .

Susan: I can't find my _____ and my _____ .

Teacher: Did anyone see Susan's _____ and _____ ?

Misha: Look in the _____ .

Teacher: Where did you put your _____ and _____ ?

Susan: I put them on the _____ with my _____ and _____ .

Teacher: Look in the _____ , too.

Andre: I found them.

Teacher: Where were they?

Andre: They were in the _____ .

Exercise 6 Make up five questions about the dialogue and then answer them.

1. Q. _____ ?
   A. _____ .
2. Q. _____ ?
   A. _____ .
3. Q. _____ ?
   A. _____ .

4. Q. _____ ?

   A. _____ .

5. Q. _____ ?

   A. _____ .

Lesson **14** The New Student

Exercise 1   Read the dialogue.

Yves: Did you see the new girl in Mrs. Rein's class?

Peter: Yes, I did.

Yves: What's her name?

Peter: Her name's Lin.

Renée: Where is she from?

Peter: She's from China.

Renée: How old is she?

Peter: She's 16 years old.

Yves: She seems very nice.

Peter: Yes, and she's a good student, too.

Exercise 2   Complete each sentence with a word or phrase from the list below.

very nice	new girl	a good student	I did	years old
is she	class	name	see her	China

1. Who's the _____ ?

2. What's her _____ ?

3. She seems _____ .

4. She's _____ .

5. How old _____ ?

6. She's from _____ .

7. She's sixteen _____ .

8. She's in Mrs. Rein's _____ .

9. Did you _____ .

10. Yes, _____ .

Exercise 3   Complete the dialogue.

    Arnie: Who's the new boy in our class?

   Akouvi: _____

    Arnie: What's his name?

   Akouvi: _____

    Arnie: Where is he from?

   Akouvi: _____

    Arnie: How old is he?

   Akouvi: _____

    Arnie: Let's talk to him after school.

   Akouvi: Good idea.

Exercise 4   Complete the dialogue so that it tells about your school.

New Student: Excuse me. I'm new here. Can you tell me where the cafeteria is?

      You: _____

             _____

New Student: Where do I go if I want a book? or if I need help?

      You: _____

             _____

New Student: And where do I go to speak to the principal?

      You: _____

             _____

New Student: Are you busy later? Maybe we can play some basketball. Where do we go for that?

      You: _____

             _____

New Student: Thanks for helping me. I feel more at home now. Can you direct me to the nurse? I need a medical examination for the school.

You: _____

_____

New Student: O.K. See you at three o'clock.

Exercise 5 Find and circle the hidden words. Look across, down, diagonally, forward, and backward. Then find the nine letters you do not use. Unscramble them to find the mystery word. Write the mystery word below the puzzle.

address	chair	door	lunch	restroom
ask	chalk	eraser	notebook	ruler
athletic	class	exam	office	school
auditorium	closet	girl	paints	seat
bell	coat hooks	gym	pens	stenography
book	country	ink	pencils	teachers
cabinet	crayon	library	pictures	telephone
cafeteria	desk	lights	read	test
				wall

L	C	M	C	T	P	I	C	T	U	R	E	S	K	L	A	H	C
I	O	O	O	A	S	L	L	C	A	M	C	R	P	B	L	P	A
G	A	O	U	E	T	U	O	A	T	A	L	E	E	E	R	A	B
H	T	R	N	S	E	N	S	F	H	X	A	H	N	L	I	I	I
T	H	T	T	E	N	C	E	E	L	E	S	C	C	L	G	N	N
S	O	S	R	N	O	H	T	T	E	N	S	A	I	Y	P	T	E
S	O	E	Y	O	G	C	E	E	T	L	O	E	L	R	T	S	T
S	K	R	K	H	R	E	C	R	I	O	R	T	S	A	E	C	N
E	S	S	R	P	A	R	I	I	C	O	I	D	E	R	S	R	I
R	E	S	N	E	P	A	F	A	L	H	A	A	A	B	T	A	B
D	W	A	L	L	H	S	F	I	G	C	H	E	S	I	O	Y	O
D	O	O	R	E	Y	E	O	P	Y	S	C	R	K	L	A	O	O
A	U	D	I	T	O	R	I	U	M	R	U	L	E	R	I	N	K

Mystery Word: __P__ __ __ __ __ __ __ __ __

Lesson **15** **Review of the School**

Exercise 1   Complete these sentences so that they tell about you.

1. My name is _____ .

2. I'm from _____ .

3. I live in _____ .

4. My address is _____ .

5. My telephone number is _____ .

6. I go to school at _____ .

7. I'm in the _____ grade.

8. My English teacher's name is _____ .

9. I eat lunch in the _____ .

10. I study and check out books in the _____ .

Exercise 2   Write the correct words on the lines below the pictures.

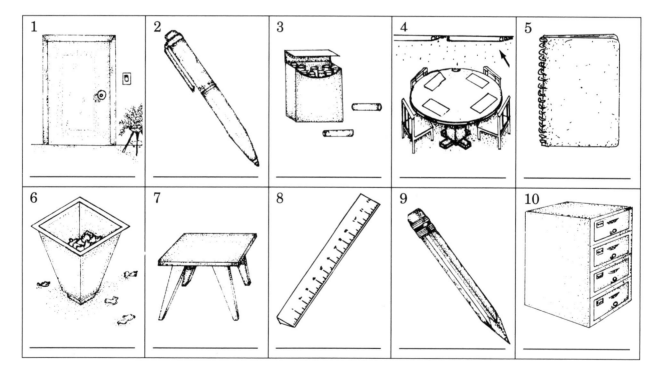

Exercise 3   Complete the sentences.

1. When we're hot, we open a _____ .

2. We walk into a room through the _____ .

3. We write on the _____ with chalk.

4. Each student sits **at** a _____ .

5. Each student sits **on** a _____ .

6. There are many _____ on a wall.

7. We hang our coats on _____ .

8. Extra books and materials are in the _____ .

9. We color with _____ .

10. We read from our _____ .

Exercise 4   Read the sentences and write **True** or **False** on the line next to each one.

1. We eat in the library.   _____

2. We play soccer in the restroom.   _____

3. We get paint from the nurse.   _____

4. We hear concerts in the auditorium.   _____

5. We get help with our problems from the
   guidance counselor.   _____

6. We speak to the principal on the athletic field. _____

7. We get books in the library.   _____

8. If we feel sick, we go to see the nurse.   _____

9. We play basketball in the art room.   _____

10. We do exercises in the gym.   _____

Exercise 5   Make up a dialogue between two students about their school. Then write
five questions about your dialogue. Have your classmates read the
dialogue and answer the questions.

Dialogue

_____

_____

_____

_____

_____

_____

_____

_____

_____

_____

_____

_____

_____

Questions

1. _____

   _____

2. _____

   _____

3. _____

   _____

4. _____

   _____

5. _____

   _____

Exercise 6   Add the suggested letters to make new words. You may need to rearrange the letters in the old words to make the new ones.

1. widow + n = _____   6. sight + l = _____

2. rod   + o = _____   7. colts + e = _____

3. late   + b = _____   8. rule   + r = _____

4. rich   + a = _____   9. all   + w = _____

5. lack   + h = _____   10. sure + n = _____

Exercise 7   Write a dialogue that takes place in the library, cafeteria, nurse's office, gym, or principal's office of a school. Then write five questions about your dialogue for the class to answer.

Dialogue

_____

_____

_____

_____

_____

_____

_____

_____

_____

_____

Questions

1. _____

_____

2. _____

_____

3. _____

_____

4. _____

_____

5. _____

_____

Exercise 8   Complete the crossword puzzle.

Across

1 We check out books from a _____ .

3 We sit in _____ .

5 A person who studies at school is a _____ .

8 We go to school five days a _____ .

9 The abbreviation for et cetera is _____ .

10 I like to read _____ about animals.

13 Our _____ often give us homework.

16 The basketball player is very _____ .

19 Wear a shirt and a _____ to the party. It's formal.

21 Girls sometimes wear _____ up.

23 The past tense of **do** is _____ .

24 Write your homework in your _____ .

28 Please _____ what's on the chalkboard.

30 The principal is in his _____ .

31 There are many pictures on those _____ .

Down

2 We go to concerts in the _____ .

3 We write on the board with _____ .

4 Use a _____ to make a straight line.

5 We study at _____ .

6 There are four chairs around the _____ .

7 If the room is dark, turn on the _____ .

11 We read, write, and _____ English.

12 If you want to use a computer, you should learn to _____ .

14 We eat lunch in the _____ .

15 Please _____ in the chair.

17 The school bell is very _____ .

18 Sharpen your _____ .

20 The _____ in my pen is blue.

22 There is one _____ leading into my room.

23 I feel a _____ . Please close the window.

25 We play with a _____ in gym class.

26 Use a blue _____ to write your essay.

27 Meet the _____ student.

28 The abbreviation for exercise is _____ .

29 She likes to paint in _____ class.

Everyday English, Book Two

Unit 4 Money

Lesson 16 U.S. Currency

Exercise 1   Study these sentences and pictures with your teacher.

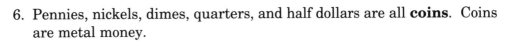

1. A **penny** is worth one cent.

2. A **nickel** is worth five cents.

3. A **dime** is worth ten cents.

4. A **quarter** is worth twenty-five cents.

5. A **half dollar** is worth fifty cents.

6. Pennies, nickels, dimes, quarters, and half dollars are all **coins**. Coins are metal money.

7. Another word for coins is **change**.

Exercise 2   Match the words in column A with the definitions in column B.

A	B
____ 1. coins	a. fifty cents
____ 2. penny	b. change
____ 3. half dollar	c. one cent
____ 4. quarter	d. twenty-five cents
____ 5. dime	e. five cents
____ 6. nickel	f. ten cents

Exercise 3   Study this paragraph with your teacher.

A **bill** is paper money. Bills are usually worth more than coins. Here are some U.S. bills:

one-dollar bill

five-dollar bill

ten-dollar bill

twenty-dollar bill

fifty-dollar bill

one-hundred-dollar bill

Some bills are worth more than one hundred dollars, but they are not used very often by most people. A **buck** is a slang word for a dollar.

Exercise 4   If you don't have any bills, you can use change to make a dollar. Complete the sentences with words from the list below.

pennies   nickels   dimes   quarters   half dollars

Example: Two _____half dollars_____ equal one dollar.

1. Ten _____ equal one dollar.

2. One hundred _____ equal one dollar.

3. Four _____ equal one dollar.

4. Twenty _____ equal one dollar.

Exercise 5   Study this dialogue with your teacher.

José Luís: Excuse me, can I have change for a buck?

Laurette: Of course. Here's a dollar

José Luís: No. I need change.

Laurette: You want me to change a dollar? How do you want me to change it? I'm not a magician.

José Luís: I want change *for* a dollar. I need coins for the parking meter and the washing machine.

Laurette: Oh, I understand. Here . . . (She starts counting one hundred pennies.)

José Luís: No, no, I need ten dimes, four quarters, or twenty nickels. I can use five dimes and two quarters; or three dimes, four nickels, and two quarters. Better yet, three quarters, two dimes, and a nickel.

Laurette: Oh, I see. But I only have pennies and a one-dollar bill. Do you have change?

José Luís: Never mind. I'll ask somebody else.

Exercise 6   Complete the sentences.

1. José Luís asks Laurette for _____ .

2. Laurette gives him _____ .

3. José Luís doesn't _____ it. He needs _____

   _____ .

4. Laurette _____ understand at first.

5. José Luís needs _____ for the _____

   _____ and the _____ .

6. Laurette starts counting _____ .

7. José Luís needs _____ dimes, four _____ ,

   or twenty _____ .

8. He can also use _____ dimes and _____ quarters;

   or three _____ , four _____ , and

   _____ quarters.

9. Laurette only has _____ and a _____ .

10. José Luís decides to _____ .

Lesson **17** Counting Money

Exercise 1

The dollar sign (**$**) and the cent sign (**¢**) are two symbols we use when we write amounts of money. Look at these sentences and pictures.

- Giselle has seventy-five cents.
- Giselle has 75¢

- The notebook costs one dollar and fifty-nine cents.
- The notebook costs $1.59.

Look at each group of coins and bills. Circle the answer that shows the correct amount of money.

1.

   a. $1.24   b. $1.59   c. $1.39

2.

   a. 98¢   b. 85¢   c. $1.35

3.

   a. $20.26   b. $10.26   c. $20.06

4.

   a. 61¢   b. 71¢   c. $1.11

5.

   a. $2.41   b. $10.67   c. $10.41

Everyday English, Book Two

Exercise 2   Write the total amount of money for each group of coins and bills.

Example: two nickels and one dime   20¢

1. a buck fifty   _____

2. four pennies, two quarters, and two dimes   _____

3. half a buck   _____

4. two half dollars   _____

5. three dimes, two nickels, and one quarter   _____

Exercise 3   Circle the greater amount of money

1.   a. two dimes   b. eighteen pennies

2.   a. one quarter   b. two dimes

3.   a. three dimes   b. one dime and five pennies

4.   a. five dimes   b. four dimes and five pennies

5.   a. four quarters   b. eight dimes and ten pennies

Exercise 4   Fill in the price tag for each amount of money.

Example: one dime and two pennies   12¢

1. four quarters and one dime

2. four dimes and seven pennies

3. six dimes and six pennies

4. a half dollar and two nickels.

5. three dimes and twelve quarters.

Unit 4 Money   49

6. one dollar and seventeen pennies

7. seven dimes and nine nickels

8. eight half dollars

9. three nickels and three quarters

10. six dimes and five nickels.

Exercise 5   Complete the sentences.

1. One dime and _____ pennies make thirteen cents.

2. _____ dimes and five pennies make forty-five cents.

3. Two quarters and one half dollar equal _____ .

4. Eight nickels and _____ dimes equal one dollar.

5. _____ nickels and eight half dollars make four dollars and eighty cents.

Lesson **18** **Talking about Money**

Exercise 1   Write at least three combinations of bills and coins that equal each amount of money.

Example: 10¢   _2 nickels; 10 pennies; 1 dime;_

1 nickel and 5 pennies

1.   25¢   _____

_____

2.   50¢   _____

_____

3. $1.00   _____

_____

_____

4.   35¢   _____

_____

5.   75¢   _____

_____

6.   63¢   _____

_____

7.   87¢   _____

_____

8. $1.25   _____

_____

_____

9.   98¢   _____

_____

10. $5.49   _____

_____

Exercise 2   Read this paragraph with your teacher.

When you buy something and pay for it with bills or coins, you are paying **cash**. If you don't have a combination of bills and coins that exactly equals the price of the item, you may give the salesperson too much money. He or she will then give some money back to you. The money you get back is called **change**. (This is a second meaning for *change*.) Look at this example:

Katrina is buying a pair of shoes. The total price is $23.60. Katrina gives the salesman $25.00 — a twenty-dollar bill and a five-dollar bill. He gives her back $1.40 — a one-dollar bill, a quarter, a dime, and a nickel. Her change is $1.40, because:

$25.00   — $23.60   = $1.40
(what she paid)   (price of the shoes)   (her change)

Exercise 3   Look at the price of each item and the amount of money the customer paid for it. Tell how much change the customer will get.

	Price	Payment	Change
Example:	37¢	40¢	3¢
1.	81¢	$1.00	_____
2.	$1.29	$1.30	_____
3.	$1.35	$1.50	_____
4.	96¢	$1.06	_____
5.	$2.07	$2.25	_____
6.	$6.95	$7.00	_____
7.	$7.29	$8.00	_____
8.	$9.91	$10.01	_____
9.	$15.63	$15.75	_____
10.	$16.30	$20.00	_____

Exercise 4   Read this dialogue.

Consuela: I'd like to buy this sweater.

Salesperson: O.K. That will be $33.71 with tax.

Consuela: I'll pay cash. Here's $35.00.

Salesperson: Thank you. Your change is $1.29.

Consuela: Thanks.

Salesperson: Here's your sweater. Come again soon.

Consuela: I'm sure I will. Bye.

Salesperson: Good-bye.

Everyday English, Book Two

Exercise 5   Answer these questions in complete sentences.

1. What's a bill?_____

2. What's a quarter?_____

3. What's a dime? _____

4. What's a nickel? _____

5. What's a buck? _____

6. What's a coin? _____

7. What's cash? _____

Lesson 19 Review of Money

Exercise 1   Tell how much money each person has.

Example: Laura has a quarter, a dime, and two pennies.

She has _____37¢_____ .

1. Clare has a one-dollar bill, two dimes, and three nickels. He has

   _____ .

2. Martina has a half dollar, two quarters, and four pennies. She has

   _____ .

3. José has a ten-dollar bill, four dimes, a nickel, and five pennies. He

   has _____ .

4. Kirsten has ten dimes and two nickels. She has

   _____ .

5. Nicole has a five-dollar bill and twenty nickels. She has

   _____ .

Exercise 2   Solve the problems.

Example: Stefan paid $8.00 for a book. The price of the book was $7.79.

Stefan's change was _____21¢_____ .

1. Karl paid 25¢ for a pencil. The price of the pencil was 19¢. Karl's

   change was _____ .

2. Zaratou paid $12.03 for a scarf. The price of the scarf was $11.83.

   Zaratou's change was _____ .

3. Kenji paid 90¢ for an eraser. The price of the eraser was 81¢. Kenji's

   change was _____ .

4. Miyoko paid $1.50 for a pen. The price of the pen was $1.29. Miyoko's

   change was _____ .

5. Tenena paid $22.99 for a shirt. The price of the shirt was $22.99.

   Tenena's change was _____ .

Exercise 3   The word going down is COIN. Write a money word going across each
letter in COIN.

N I C K E L
__ O __ __ __ __
__ I __ __
__ __ N __ __

Exercise 4   Unscramble the words at the left. Write one letter in each box at the
right. Then unscramble the letters in the circles to spell out the mystery
word.

1. e i m d

2. r l o a d l

3. n e y n p

4. e l k n c i

5. g n h a c e

Mystery Word: ___ ___ ___ ___ ___

Unit 5 Transportation

Lesson 20 Methods of Transportation

Exercise 1   Write the correct words on the lines below the pictures. Choose words from this list.

airplane	boat	car	motorcycle	train
bicycle	bus	helicopter	taxi	truck

1 _____

2 _____

3 _____

4 _____

5 _____

6 _____

7 _____

8 _____

9 _____

10 _____

Exercise 2   Unscramble the words at the left. Write one letter in each box at the right. Then unscramble the letters in the circles to spell out the mystery word.

1. l e p a n r i a

2. a r e

3. k r c u t

4. a t o b

5. e b i y l c c

Mystery Word: ___ ___ ___ ___ ___

Exercise 3   Unscramble these methods of transportation.

1. n a r i t _____

2. a t o b _____

3. s u b _____

4. a r c _____

5. recelophit _____

6. a x i t _____

7. p a l i r n e a _____

8. c u r t k _____

9. corcletmoy _____

10. c y b l i e c _____

Now alphabetize the words you unscrambled.

_____

_____

_____

_____

_____

_____

_____

_____

_____

_____

Exercise 4   Look at the pictures and complete the sentences.

1. To go from building A to building B, we could use a _____ ,

_____ , _____ , or _____ .

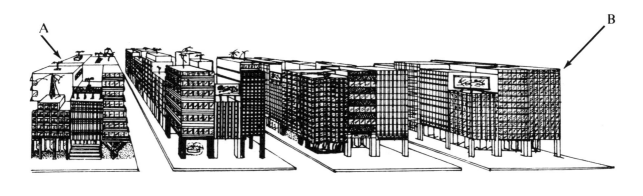

2. To go from Florida to Spain, we could use an _____ or

a _____ .

3. To go from Maine to California, we could use an _____ ,

_____ , _____ , or _____ .

4. We use a _____ , _____ , _____ ,

_____ , or _____ to travel on a highway.

Other words for **highway** are route, freeway, expressway, parkway, and throughway.

Exercise 5   Talk about these sentences and pictures with your teacher.

A bridge is built over water to connect two pieces of land.

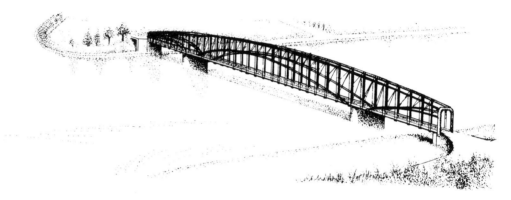

A tunnel is built under the water to connect two pieces of land. Some tunnels go through mountains.

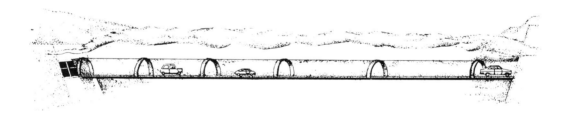

Exercise 6   Answer these questions in complete sentences.

1. What travels on land? _____

_____

2. What travels in the water? _____

_____

3. What travels in the air? _____

_____

4. What travels on tracks? _____

_____

5. What goes over water to connect two pieces of land? _____

_____

6. What goes under water to connect two pieces of land? _____

_____

7. Is an ocean large or small? _____

Can we build a bridge over an ocean, or a tunnel under one? _____

_____ Why or why not? _____

_____

8. What vehicles can travel on a highway? _____

_____

9. Do you need a license to ride a bicycle? _____

_____

10. Do we usually travel by plane to a place that is not far away? _____

_____

Exercise 7   Match the synonyms. Write the correct letter from column B next to each number in column A.

A	B
_____ 1. boat	a. expressway
_____ 2. highway	b. bike
_____ 3. bicycle	c. ship
_____ 4. airplane	d. cab
_____ 5. taxi	e. plane

Exercise 8   Add the suggested letters to make new words. You may need to rearrange the letters in the old words to make the new ones.

1. l a n e + p = _____

2. t a x + i = _____

3. b a t + o = _____

4. s i p + h = _____

5. r a i n + t = _____

6. c u r t + k = _____

7. d i r g e + b = _____

8. t o u r + e = _____

9. c o n e + a = _____

10. r a t e + w = _____

Exercise 9   Circle the best answer for each sentence.

1. Maguette flew in a _____ .

   a. boat   b. plane

2. Justin rode **in** a _____ .

   a. taxi   b. motorcycle

3. Pavl rode **on** a _____ .

   a. bicycle   b. truck

4. Ariel sailed in a _____ .

   a. helicopter   b. ship

Exercise 10   Choose one way of traveling that you like and write a few sentences about it. Tell why you like it. Describe what it looks like and how it works. Tell about a time you traveled this way, or tell where you would like to travel in this type of vehicle.

_____

_____

_____

_____

_____

_____

_____

_____

_____

_____

_____

Lesson **21** **Traveling by Air**

Exercise 1   Look at this picture of an airport terminal. Discuss the picture with your teacher and see how many things in the picture you can name.

_____   _____

_____   _____

_____   _____

_____   _____

_____   _____

_____   _____

_____   _____

_____   _____

_____   _____

Exercise 2   Match the words in column A with the definitions in column B.

A	B
____ 1. one-way	a. to make a reservation
____ 2. round-trip	b. a note that allows someone to get money from your bank account
____ 3. flight	c. leaving the ground
____ 4. to book	d. going and coming
____ 5. fare	e. suitcases and other bags
____ 6. a check	f. to get on a plane
____ 7. to check baggage	g. the price of a ticket
____ 8. taking off	h. going somewhere and not returning
____ 9. to board	i. to register your luggage with the airline company
____ 10. luggage	j. a trip on a plane

Exercise 3   Read the dialogue. You can change the underlined words to make the dialogue tell about you.

Travel Agent: May I help you?

John: Yes. I would like a plane ticket to Paris, France, on Wide World Airlines.

Travel Agent: Is that one-way or round-trip?

John: Round-trip, please.

Travel Agent: Do you want first class or tourist class?

John: Tourist class.

Travel Agent: When would you like to leave?

John: I'd like to leave on Thursday, June 29, and return on Monday, August 14.

Travel Agent: Our flights are full on those days. Would a flight on Friday, June 30, returning Tuesday, August 15, be all right?

John: Yes, I think so.

Travel Agent: Good. I can book you for those flights. You'll leave from <u>Kennedy Airport</u> on Friday, June 30. Boarding time is 9:00 P.M., and takeoff is at 10:00 P.M. The return flight will be on <u>Tuesday, August 15</u>, from <u>De Gaulle Airport</u>. Ask in <u>Paris</u> for the correct boarding and takeoff times. Don't forget to call <u>Wide World</u> to confirm your flight three days in advance. Check your baggage at the airport one hour before boarding time.

John: How much if the fare?

Travel Agent: That will be <u>five hundred dollars</u>, round-trip. Will you pay in cash or by check?

John: Here's a <u>check</u>. Thanks very much. Bye.

Travel Agent: Have a good trip.

Exercise 4   Complete these sentences about the dialogue.

1. John wants a _____ to Paris.

2. He wants a _____ ticket.

3. He will fly _____ class.

4. Boarding time is one hour before _____ .

5. He should check his baggage _____ before boarding.

Exercise 5   Answer these questions about the dialogue. Use complete sentences.

1. How much is the fare? _____

_____

2. Does John pay in cash or by check?_____

_____

What is cash? _____

What is a check?_____

_____

3. When must John confirm his flight?_____

_____

4. Which is cheaper, tourist class or first class? _____

_____

5. What days will John be traveling?_____

_____

Exercise 6   Put these sentences in the correct order to tell the story.

_____ The agent asks him when he wants to leave.

_____ The agent tells him that day is booked.

_____ John goes to the travel agent. He wants to book a flight.

_____ John wants to leave on June 29.

_____ John agrees to leave on June 30.

Exercise 7   Unscramble the words at the left. Write one letter in each box at the right. Then unscramble the letters in the circles to spell out the mystery word.

1. g e g u g a l

2. h e c c k

3. d o n u r   p r i t

4. u i t s e c a s

5. a g e a g b g

6. a r e f

Mystery Word: ___ ___ ___ ___ ___ ___

Lesson 22 Traveling by Bus

Exercise 1 Match the words in column A with the definitions in column B.

A
B

____ 1. waiting room

a. getting on the bus

____ 2. boarding

b. a person who carries your luggage for you

____ 3. suitcases

c. the place where tickets are sold

____ 4. porter

d. a place where you sit until it is time to board the bus

____ 5. ticket window

e. luggage

Exercise 2 Talk about this picture of a bus station. Then read the paragraphs below.

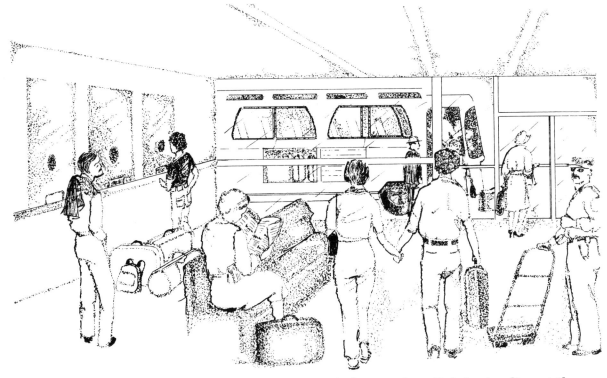

This is the waiting room at a bus station. Bob is standing at the ticket window. He is buying tickets for himself and his friend Joe. Joe is watching the luggage. He is looking for a porter to take the buggage to the bus. The suitcases are very heavy. Some people are reading newspapers while they wait. One bus is coming in, and another is leaving. Some people are boarding a bus to leave. Joe hopes it's not his bus.

Bob comes back with the tickets. He says the fare isn't too expensive. They must wait an hour until the bus leaves. Luckily, the waiting room isn't full of people, so Joe and Bob can sit down and relax.

Exercise 3   Answer these questions in complete sentences.

1. Where are Joe and Bob? _____

2. Who is buying the tickets? _____

3. Where is he buying the tickets? _____

   _____

4. What is Joe doing? _____

5. Who is he looking for? _____

6. What are some people doing? _____

   _____

7. Is the fare expensive? _____

8. How long must Joe and Bob wait for the bus? _____

   _____

9. What can Bob and Joe do while they wait? _____

   _____

10. Are the suitcases heavy? _____

Exercise 4   Fill in the blanks to complete the story.

This is the _____ _____ at the bus

_____ . Bob is standing at the _____

_____ . He is _____ tickets for himself and his

_____ Joe.   Joe is watching the _____ . He is

looking for a _____ to take the _____ to

the_____ . The _____ are very heavy. Some people

are reading _____ while they wait. One bus is _____

_____ , and another is _____ . Some people are

_____ a bus to leave. Joe hopes it's not his _____ .

Bob comes _____ with the _____ . He says the

_____ isn't too _____ . They must _____

an hour until the _____ _____ . Luckily, the

_____ _____ isn't full of _____ , so Joe

and Bob can _____ _____ and _____ .

Exercise 5   Complete this dialogue. Nari sees her friend Jim at the bus station.

Nari: Hi, Jim, what are you doing here?

Jim: _____

Nari: I'm going there, too. Have you bought your ticket yet?

Jim: _____

Nari: I just got mine. It was expensive!

Jim: _____

Nari: When are you coming back?

Jim: _____

Nari: Well, I guess I'll see you on the way back, too. Let's sit next to each other.

Jim: _____

Nari: O.K. Now all we have to do is wait. Let's sit in the waiting room and relax.

Lesson 23 Traffic Signs and Rules

Exercise 1   Study these pictures and paragraphs with your teacher.

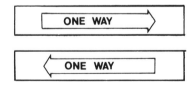

When you see this sign, you may go only right or only left. All cars go the same way on a street with this sign. This sign is black and white.

This sign tells you that the street ends. You cannot go that way to get on another street. This sign is yellow and black.

When you see this sign, you must stop completely. This sign is red with white letters.

This is a traffic light. Red (stop) is on the top. Yellow (prepare to stop) is in the middle. Green (go) is on the bottom.

When you see this sign, you must either continue straight ahead or turn left. You may not turn right. This sign is white, black, and red. There is a sign similar to this one, with the arrow pointing left. That sign, of course, means "No left turn."

Exercise 2   Draw pictures of these traffic signs and signals.

1. one-way sign	2. traffic light	3. stop sign	4. dead-end sign	5. no-right-turn sign

Exercise 3   Study these pictures and paragraphs.

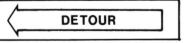

This sign tells you that the road ahead is closed for repair and that you must follow the arrow to continue. A detour means you will take the long way around. This sign is black and white.

When you see this sign, you are coming to a railroad track. Prepare to stop because a train may be coming. This sign is yellow and black.

This sign tells you to slow down and prepare to stop. The other cars or pedestrians have the right-of-way. This sign is usually white and red. Sometimes it is black and yellow.

When you see this sign, you know you can get off the expressway in one mile. Be sure you are in the correct lane if you want to exit.

This means that you may not leave your car in a particular place — for example, in front of a driveway or a bus stop.

Exercise 4   Draw pictures of these traffic signs and signals.

1. detour sign	2. railroad-crossing sign	3. yield sign	4. exit sign	5. no-parking sign

Exercise 5   Explain why you got a ticket.

1. You left your car in front of a bus stop. _____

_____

2. You did not slow down for other cars and pedestrians. _____

_____

3. You turned the wrong way onto a one-way street. _____

_____

4. You didn't stop at a busy corner. _____

_____

Now draw pictures of the signs you disobeyed.

1.	2.	3.	4.

Exercise 6   Match the words in column A with the definitions in column B.

A	**B**
____ 1. pedestrian	a. a written notice of your penalty for disobeying a traffic law
____ 2. ticket	b. a short private road leading from a street to a building, parking lot, or garage
____ 3. fire hydrant	c. permission to continue
____ 4. right-of-way	d. a person who is walking
____ 5. driveway	e. a pump where a firefighter gets water to put out fires

Exercise 7   Answer these questions in complete sentences.

1. What should you do when you see a railroad-crossing sign?_____

_____

2. What does a detour sign tell you? _____

_____

3. Which sign tells you that you can leave the expressway? _____

_____

4. What happens when you disobey a traffic sign?_____

_____

5. What do we call a street that does not go through to another street?

_____

Lesson **24** **Review of Transportation**

Exercise 1   Answer these questions in complete sentences.

1. How do you get to school? _____

_____

2. What are five methods of transportation? _____

_____

3. a. What can we build over water to connect two pieces of land?

_____

   b. What can we build under water to connect two pieces of land?

_____

4. What are two synonyms for the word **highway**?_____

_____

5. What is a round-trip ticket? _____

_____

6. What is **boarding**? _____

_____

7. What should you do when you see a yield sign?_____

_____

8. Where do you see traffic signs? _____

_____

9. What happens if you disobey a traffic sign? _____

_____

10. What is a one-way street? _____

_____

Exercise 2   Match the words in column A with the definitions in column B.

A	B
____ 1. airplane	a. ship
____ 2. traffic	b. expressway
____ 3. car	c. terminal
____ 4. railroad	d. plane
____ 5. boat	e. leave
____ 6. take off	f. auto
____ 7. pedestrians	g. train
____ 8. fare	h. cars, trucks, buses, and other vehicles on a street
____ 9. station	i. people walking
____ 10. highway	j. the cost of a ticket

Exercise 3   Write **T** if a sentence is true. Write **F** it is false.

1. A plane travels on land and sea.   _____

2. An ocean is very big.   _____

3. We sail on land.   _____

4. A porter will carry your baggage for you.   _____

5. Tourist class is the same thing as first class.   _____

6. The bottom light of a traffic light is yellow.   _____

7. If you have time before your flight leaves, you can sit in the waiting room and relax.   _____

8. A dead-end street is a street that does not go through to another street.   _____

9. The red light of a traffic light is at the top.   _____

10. Traffic goes in two directions on a one-way street.   _____

Exercise 4   Complete this dialogue.

Police officer: Pull over to the curb.

You: _____

Police officer: You just went through a red light.

You: _____

Police officer: I don't care what your excuse is. You broke the law, and you're getting a ticket.

You: _____

Police officer: Next time be careful and watch where you're going.

You: _____

Police officer: You should pay the fine as soon as you can.

You: _____

Exercise 5   Unscramble the words at the left. Write one letter in each box at the right. Then unscramble the letters in the circles to spell out the mystery word.

1. d o a r

2. l a n e p

3. f t a r f c i

4. e u r d o t

5. i r e d b g

6. a r e f

7. o n   r i n k p g a

8. o d u n r   p r i t

9. n e o   a w y

10. p o t s

11. o d a i g b n r

12. i r a t n

13. t x i e

14. a t k e   f f o

Mystery Word: __ __ __ __ __ __ __ __ __ __ __ __ __ __

Unit 5 Transportation

73

Exercise 6   Complete the crossword puzzle.

Across

1 All the traffic goes in one direction on a
  _____ - _____ street.

4 Cars, buses, and trucks are part of the
  _____ on a street.

8 Yesterday I _____ my car with gas at the
  gas station.

10 Drivers _____ behind the steering wheel.

11 A policeman writes tickets with a _____ .

12 A _____ is the long way around.

14 The top light on a traffic light is _____ .

16 The sign by that driveway says "No _____
   _____ ."

17 A synonym for **street** is _____ .

20 You must yield when other cars have the
   right-of-_____ .

22 A synonym for **car** is _____ .

23 When you drive too fast, you _____
   gasoline.

24 When you _____ in a car, always put on
   your seat belt.

25 The bottom light on a traffic light is
   _____ .

26 Wear sunglasses in the _____ .

27 People who are walking are called _____ .

Down

2 An _____ is where you can get off the
  expressway.

3 When you _____ , you slow down and
  prepare to stop.

5 Slow down and watch for a train at a
  _____ crossing.

6 You don't have to pay a _____ to travel in
  your own car.

7 Never park your _____ in front of a fire
  hydrant.

8 Firefighters get water from _____ _____

9 A red and white octagonal sign is a _____ sign.

11 Don't _____ in front of a bus stop.

13 Always yield when other cars have the _____ - _____ -way.

15 Someone who drives a car is a _____ .

18 A street that ends is a _____ - _____ street.

19 If you want to leave the expressway, make sure you're in the exit _____ .

21 [sign] This sign means no _____ turn.

Exercise 7   Write a sentence with each of these words.

1. drive _____

_____

2. park _____

_____

3. fine _____

_____

4. detour _____

_____

5. yield _____

_____

Exercise 8   Find and circle the hidden words. Look across, down, diagonally, forward, and backward. Then find the letters you do not use. Unscramble them to find the mystery word that has something to do with transportation. Write the mystery word below the puzzle.

T	I	C	K	E	T	T	I	X	E
O	C	C	Y	L	Y	I	E	L	D
L	L	A	N	E	E	L	C	A	D
E	M	R	T	N	B	D	F	N	A
S	A	S	I	N	R	N	F	I	O
W	A	F	I	U	I	E	O	M	R
R	A	G	O	T	D	D	E	R	L
O	Y	T	O	O	G	A	K	E	I
A	E	A	E	U	E	E	A	T	A
D	I	A	P	R	S	D	T	R	R

bridges   red
cars   road
dead end   sit
detour   takeoff
exit   terminal
fine   ticket
fly   tour
gas   tunnel
lane   warn
paid   water
pay   yield
railroad

Mystery Word: ___ ___ ___ ___ ___ ___ ___ ___ ___ ___

Unit 5 Transportation

75

Unit
6 Looking for an Apartment

Lesson 25 Kinds of Dwellings

Exercise 1   Unscramble the words and match them with the pictures. Write the correct word on the line above each picture.

1. epmattnar dilugnib

   a _ _ _ _ _ _ _ _   b _ _ _ _ _ _ _

2. aitprve uohse   p _ _ _ _ _ _ _ _   h _ _ _ _ _

3. expuld   d _ _ _ _ _ _

4. pramnatet omlcpxe

   a _ _ _ _ _ _ _ _ _   _ _ _ _ _ _ _

5. ovleeatr   e _ _ _ _ _ _ _ _

6. sorom   r _ _ _ _ _

7. npiacaples   a _ _ _ _ _ _ _ _ _

8. ira otdocniinign

   _ _ _   _ _ _ _ _ _ _ _ _ _ _

9. aeetbsmn   _ _ _ _ _ _ _ _

10. lpwkua   _ _ _ _ _ _

11. easel   _ _ _ _ _

12. tern   _ _ _ _

13. datenimverset

    _ _ _ _ _ _ _ _ _ _ _ _

14. gwilledsn   _ _ _ _ _ _ _ _ _

15. lofor   _ _ _ _ _

76

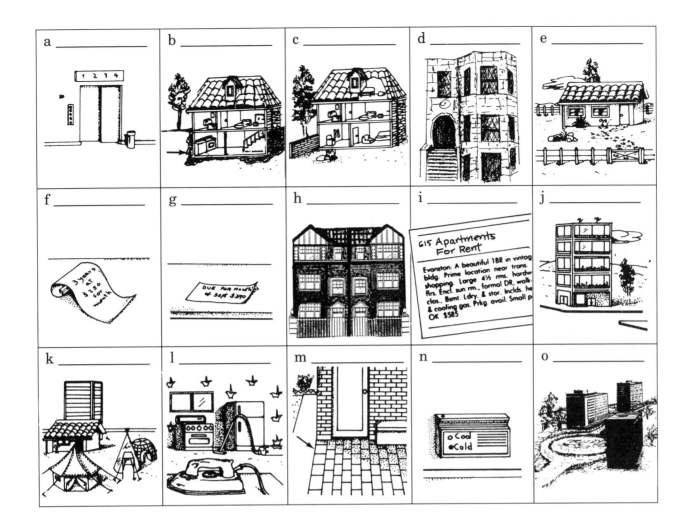

a _____

b _____

c _____

d _____

e _____

f _____

g _____

h _____

i _____

615 Apartments For Rent

Evanston: A beautiful 1BR in vintag bldg. Prime location near trans. shopping. Large 4½ rms. hardw flrs. Encl. sun rm., formal DR, walk clos., Bsmt. Ldry. & stor. Inclds. he & cooling gas. Prkg. avail. Small p OK $585

j _____

k _____

l _____

m _____

n _____

o _____

Exercise 2   How do you decide what kind of dwelling is good for you? Discuss this with your teacher. Make a list of things you should think about before choosing a place to live.

1. _____

2. _____

3. _____

4. _____

5. _____

Exercise 3   Read this ad and answer the questions about it.

> Kansas City. $4\frac{1}{2}$ rm. apt. 2 bdrm 1 bthrm,
> garage avail. nr. trans. and shopg. $350/mo.
> Call betw. 5–7 p.m. 555–9000.

1. How many rooms are in this dwelling?_____

    _____

2. Where is this dwelling located? _____

    _____

3. How can you contact the people who are advertising the apartment?

    _____

    _____

4. How many bedrooms are there?_____

    _____

5. How much is the rent? _____

    _____

6. Is there a garage? _____

    _____

7. How many bathrooms are there?_____

    _____

8. Is this dwelling for sale or for rent?_____

    _____

9. Is this dwelling near shopping and transportation? _____

    _____

Exercise 4   Read the paragraph and answer the questions.

> If you live in an apartment building, your landlord or landlady
> gives you a lease to sign. The landlord or landlady is the person who
> owns the building. The lease is a contract that tells how much rent
> you must pay for a certain period of time. Most leases are for six
> months or one year, but the rent usually must be paid every month.

1. What is a landlord or a landlady? _____

   _____

2. What is a lease? _____

   _____

3. How often must the rent be paid on an apartment? _____

   _____

Exercise 5   Complete each sentence by circling the correct answer.

1. A private house is a house in which _____ live (s).

   a. one family   b. two families

2. A group of apartment buildings that have the same landlord or

   landlady is called a _____ .

   a. duplex   b. complex

3. A little room that goes up and down and stops on each floor is an

   _____ .

   a. excavator   b. elevator

4. The money you pay for an apartment is the _____ .

   a. rent   b. lease

5. _____ keep (s) a building cool.

   a. air conditioning   b. large plants

6. If a building has no elevator, it is a _____ .

   a. staircase   b. walk-up

7. The person who owns your building is your _____ .

   a. governor   b. landlord or landlady

8. Some buildings have a _____ below the street level.

   a. cave   b. basement

9. In an _____ there are many families

   a. apartment building   b. advertisement

10. A dwelling is divided into _____ .

   a. brooms   b. rooms

Exercise 6

Read this paragraph and answer the questions.

It is important to look around before you buy a house or rent an apartment. First, decide how many rooms you want. Then decide where you want to live. Do you want a private house or a two-family house? Do you want a walk-up or an apartment building with an elevator? Do you want to live in an apartment complex where there are many families? After you answer all these questions, go out and look. Don't be disappointed if you don't find something immediately. Maybe the rent is too high, or maybe the rooms are too small. Only you can decide for yourself.

1. What should you do before you buy a house or rent an apartment?

   _____

2. What must you decide before you begin to look? _____

   _____

3. What is a walk-up? _____

   _____

4. Are there stairs in an apartment building that has an elevator?

   _____ Why? _____

   _____

5. What is an apartment complex? _____

   _____

6. Why is it sometimes difficult to find a place you like? _____

   _____

7. What are some types of dwellings other than private houses and

   apartment buildings? _____

   _____

                                             Everyday English, Book Two

Exercise 7   What kind of dwelling would you like to live in? Why? Describe the
dwelling of your dreams.

_____

_____

_____

_____

_____

_____

_____

_____

_____

_____

_____

_____

_____

_____

_____

_____

_____

_____

_____

_____

_____

_____

_____

Lesson **26** Rooms in Homes

Exercise 1   Complete the words and match them with the pictures. Write the letter of the correct picture on the line next to each word.

___ 1. b _ d r _ _ _ _

___ 2. _ i _ i _ g _ _ _ _ m

___ 3. _ _ t h _ _ _ m

___ 4. _ i _ _ h e n

___ 5. _ e _

___ 6. _ _ n _ _ g _ _ _ m

___ 7. _ t t i _

___ 8. _ a _ e _ _ _ t

___ 9. _ a r _ _ e

___ 10. _ _ r s _ _ y

Exercise 2   Study these sentences with your teacher.

1. The bedroom is for sleeping.
2. The living room is for entertaining.
3. The bathroom is for washing.
4. The kitchen is for preparing and eating food.
5. The dining room is for eating and entertaining.
6. The den is for relaxing or working.
7. The basement is for playing, parties, or storage.
8. The attic is for storing old things.
9. The garage is for the car.
10. The nursery is for the baby.

Exercise 3   Match each room with its function.

A	B
____ 1. bathroom	a. storing old things
____ 2. dining room	b. relaxing or working
____ 3. den	c. preparing and eating food
____ 4. nursery	d. keeping the car
____ 5. attic	e. sleeping
____ 6. basement	f. entertaining
____ 7. kitchen	g. eating and entertaining
____ 8. living room	h. washing
____ 9. bedroom	i. playing, parties, or storage
____ 10. garage	j. taking care of baby

Exercise 4   Answer these questions in complete sentences.

1. Which room is for eating and preparing food? _____

_____

_____

2. Which room is for sleeping?_____

_____

_____

3. Which room is for storing old things? _____

_____

_____

4. Which room is for playing, parties, or storage? _____

_____

_____

5. Which room is for the baby? _____

_____

6. Which room is for washing up? _____

_____

7. Which room is for eating and entertaining? _____

_____

8. Which room is for relaxing and working? _____

_____

9. Which room is for the car? _____

_____

10. Which room is for entertaining? _____

_____

Exercise 5   Unscramble the words at the left. Write one letter in each box at the right. Then unscramble the letters in the circles to spell out the mystery word.

1. i i g v l n   o r o m

2. m a h o b r t o

3. m d o e o b r

4. t e e a s n b m

5. e n d

Mystery Word: ___ ___ ___ ___ ___

Exercise 6   Name all the rooms in your home.

_____   _____

_____   _____

_____   _____

_____   _____

_____   _____

Exercise 7   Answer these questions about your home.

1. Where do you entertain? _____

_____

2. Where do you sleep? _____

_____

3. Where do you eat breakfast and supper? _____

_____

4. Where do you do your homework? _____

_____

5. Where do you watch TV? _____

_____

6. Where do you take a shower? _____

_____

7. Where do you keep your car? _____

_____

8. Where do you relax? _____

_____

9. Where do you get dressed? _____

_____

10. Where do you wash your hands and face? _____

_____

Lesson 27 Home Furnishings

Exercise 1 Write the correct word above each picture. Then complete the sentence.

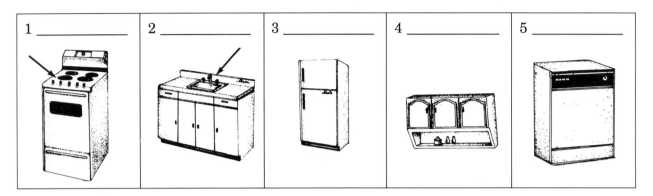

1 _____
2 _____
3 _____
4 _____
5 _____

This room is a _____ .

Exercise 2 Read these sentences with your teacher.

1. We cook on the stove.
2. We cook in the oven.
3. We keep food cold in the refrigerator.
4. We wash dishes in the sink or in the dishwasher.
5. We keep dishes, pots, and pans in the kitchen cabinets.

Exercise 3 Match the items with their functions.

A	B
____ 1. stove	a. wash dishes
____ 2. sink	b. prepare and eat food
____ 3. cabinets	c. keep food cold
____ 4. refrigerator	d. cook
____ 5. kitchen	e. keep dishes, pots, and pans

Exercise 4   Write the correct word above each picture. Then complete the sentence.

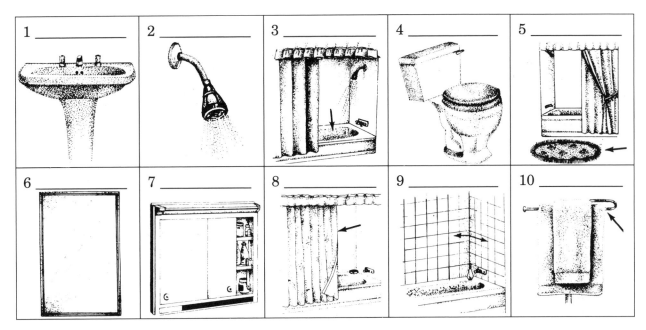

1 _____

2 _____

3 _____

4 _____

5 _____

6 _____

7 _____

8 _____

9 _____

10 _____

This room is a _____ .

Exercise 5   Study these sentences with your teacher.

1. We wash our hands and faces in the sink.
2. We take a shower or a bath in the bathtub.
3. We keep medicine in the medicine cabinet.
4. We look in the mirror when we comb our hair, shave, or put on makeup.
5. The shower curtain keeps the water from getting the floor wet.
6. The bathroom walls and floor are often made of tiles.
7. We hang our towels on the towel rack.
8. After our bath or shower, we step on the bath mat.
9. The shower head is over the bathtub.
10. We use the toilet when we have to go to the bathroom.

Exercise 6   Match the items with their functions.

A	B
____ 1. sink	a. for looking at ourselves
____ 2. medicine cabinet	b. for covering walls or floors
____ 3. shower curtain	c. for spraying water
____ 4. bath mat	d. for keeping the water inside the tub
____ 5. towel rack	e. for washing hands
____ 6. shower head	f. for stepping on after a bath.
____ 7. tile	g. for keeping medicine
____ 8. mirror	h. for hanging towels

Exercise 7   Identify this room and all the things in it.

_____   _____

_____   _____

_____   _____

_____   _____

_____   _____

_____   _____

_____   _____

_____   _____

This room is a _____ .

Exercise 8   Identify this room and all the things in it.

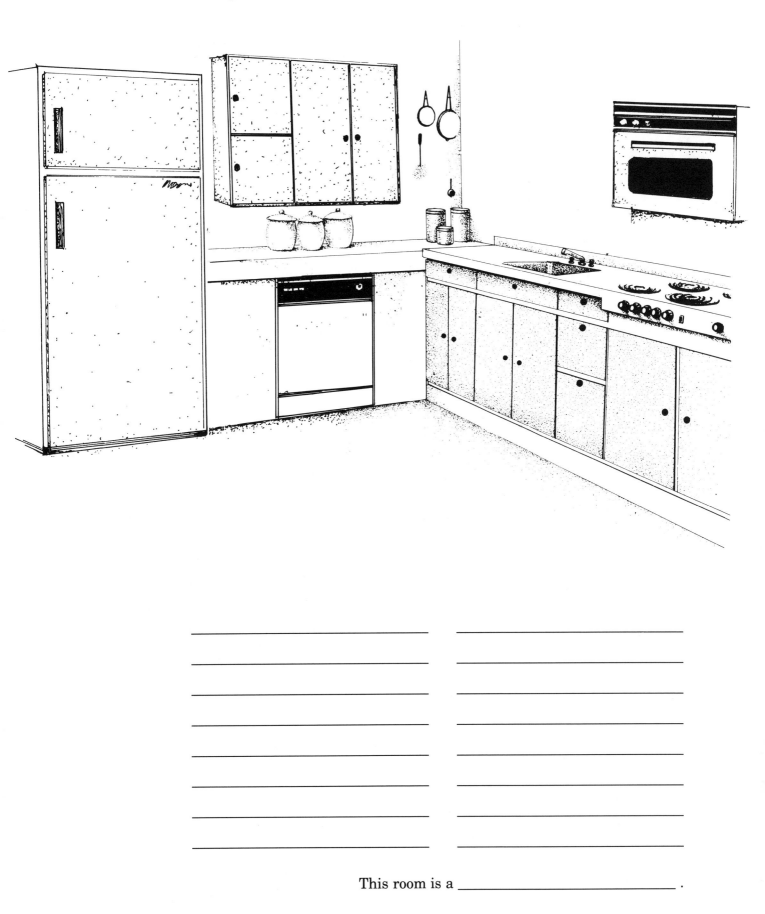

_____   _____

_____   _____

_____   _____

_____   _____

_____   _____

_____   _____

_____   _____

This room is a _____ .

Exercise 9   Write a question for each answer.

Example: On the towel rack. _____Where do we hang our towels?_____

1. In the sink. _____

2. In the mirror. _____

3. On the bath mat. _____

4. In the bathtub. _____

5. In the medicine cabinet. _____

Lesson **28** More Home Furnishings

Exercise 1   Write the correct word above each picture. Then complete the sentence.

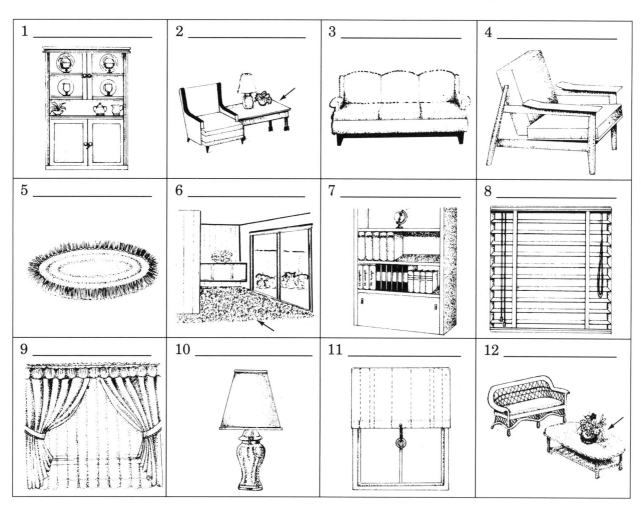

This room is a _____ .

Exercise 2   Study these sentences with your teacher.

1. We sit on a couch or in an armchair.
2. A rug is a small carpet.
3. Carpeting goes from wall to wall.
4. We put books in a bookcase.
5. Shades and venetian blinds can keep out the sunlight and prevent people from seeing through a window.
6. A lamp provides light. We often put a lamp on an end table.
7. A breakfront is a display case.
8. We can serve things to eat on a coffee table.

Exercise 3   Match the words in column A with the words in column B to make sentences.

A	**B**
____ 1. We sit on	a. goes from wall to wall.
____ 2. A rug is	b. can be opened and closed to let in or keep out sunlight.
____ 3. A bookcase	c. on a coffee table.
____ 4. Venetian blinds	d. a couch.
____ 5. A breakfront is	e. can be pulled down to keep out the sunlight.
____ 6. Shades	f. on an end table.
____ 7. A lamp	g. a small carpet.
____ 8. We often put a lamp	h. gives us light.
____ 9. Carpeting	i. a display case.
____ 10. We can serve things to eat	j. has books in it.

Exercise 4   Write the correct word above each picture. Then complete the sentence.

1 _____ 2 _____ 3 _____ 4 _____ 5 _____

This room is a _____ .

Exercise 5   Study these sentences with your teacher.
1. We sleep in a bed.
2. We have a nightstand near the bed.
3. We store folded clothing in a dresser.
4. We hang suits, dresses, shirts, skirts, and pants in a clothes closet.
5. We can comb our hair and get dressed in front of a dressing table.

Exercise 6   Match the items with their functions.

A	B
____ 1. bed	a. for storing folded clothing
____ 2. nightstand	b. for getting dressed in front of
____ 3. dresser	c. for sleeping
____ 4. closet	d. for hanging shirts, pants, and dresses
____ 5. dressing table	e. for holding a lamp and an alarm clock

Exercise 7   Name some things that can be found in any room in a home.

_____

_____

_____

_____

Exercise 8   Identify this room and all the things in it.

Everyday English, Book Two

_____   _____
_____   _____
_____   _____
_____   _____
_____   _____
_____   _____
_____   _____

This room is a _____ .

Exercise 9   Identify this room and all the things in it.

_____   _____
_____   _____
_____   _____
_____   _____
_____   _____

This room is a _____ .

Lesson **29** **Housewares**

Exercise 1   Answer these questions in complete sentences.

      1. In what room do you entertain? _____

      _____

      2. What is in this room? _____

      _____

Exercise 2   Answer these questions in complete sentences.

      1. Where does your family eat? _____

      _____

      2. What is in this room? _____

      _____

Exercise 3   Identify these kitchen items. Write the correct word above each picture.

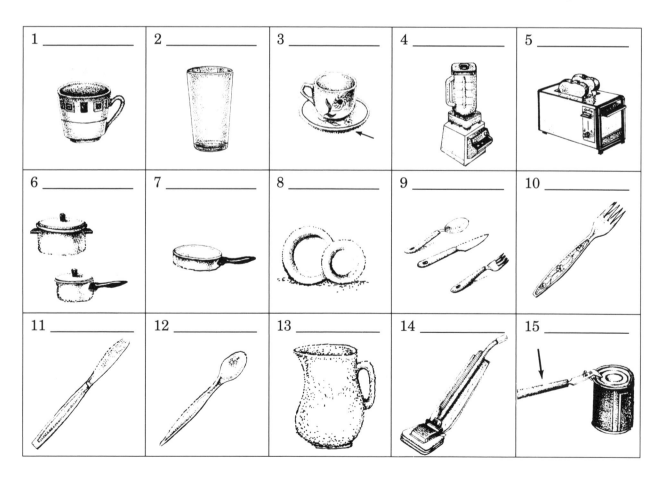

16 _____	17 _____	18 _____	19 _____	20 _____

Exercise 4   Fill in the blanks to complete the paragraphs. Use any words that make sense.

There are many things in a kitchen. We drink from a

_____ or a _____ . If we're hungry,

we put food on a _____ and eat it with

_____ . A _____ ,

_____ , and _____ are called

silverware. We wipe our fingers on a _____ .

When we cook, we use _____ and

_____ . We can prepare a meal quickly in a

_____ . If we spill something, we clean it up with a

_____ _____ . Can you name some

other things in a kitchen.

Exercise 5   Write **T** if a sentence is true. Write **F** if it is false.

1. We mop the floor with a broom.   _____

2. We open a can with a napkin.   _____

3. We put a saucer under a cup.   _____

4. We mix food in a blender.   _____

5. We fry eggs in a toaster.   _____

Exercise 6   Answer these questions in complete sentences.

1. What do you put in a kitchen cabinet? _____

_____

2. What do you put in a bedroom closet? _____

_____

3. What do you put in a hall closet? _____

_____

4. What do you put in a bathroom cabinet? _____

_____

5. What do you put in a linen closet? _____

_____

Lesson 30 More Housewares

Exercise 1   Answer these questions in complete sentences.

1. In what room do we sleep? _____

_____

2. What do we see in this room? _____

_____

Exercise 2   Write the correct word above each picture.

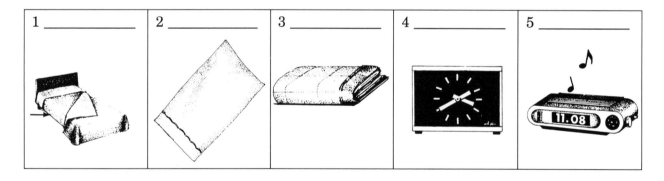

| 1 _____ | 2 _____ | 3 _____ | 4 _____ | 5 _____ |

Exercise 3   Match the words in column A with the words in column B to make sentences.

A	**B**
____ 1. A sheet	a. covers a pillow.
____ 2. A pillowcase	b. wakes you up in the morning.
____ 3. A pillow	c. is a heavy cover.
____ 4. An alarm clock	d. is where you put your head.
____ 5. A blanket	e. covers a mattress.

Everyday English, Book Two

Exercise 4   Answer these questions in complete sentences.

1. In what room do we wash our clothes?_____

_____

2. What do we see in this room? _____

_____

Exercise 5   Write the correct words the pictures.

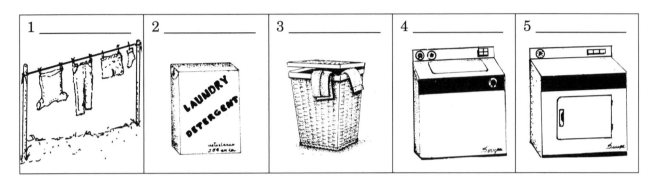

| 1 _____ | 2 _____ | 3 _____ | 4 _____ | 5 _____ |

Exercise 6   Match the words in column A with the words in column B to make sentences.

A	**B**
---- 1. A clothesline is	a. soap you use to wash dirty clothes (laundry).
---- 2. Laundry detergent is	b. in the hamper.
---- 3. We put our dirty clothes	c. uses warm air to to dry our wet clothes.
---- 4. We get our clothes clean	d. a place to hang clothes to dry.
---- 5. A dryer	e. in the washing machine.

Exercise 7   Write **T** if a sentence is true. Write **F** if it is false.

1. A dresser is where you hang clothes.   _____

2. A pillow is where you put your head at night.   _____

3. An alarm clock wakes you up in the morning.   _____

4. A sheet goes on the towel rack.   _____

5. A dryer gets your clothes clean.   _____

6. A blanket is under the bed.   _____

7. Laundry detergent is for washing clothes. _____

8. You put clean clothes in a hamper. _____

Exercise 8   Which room in your home do you like best? Describe it and tell why you like it.

_____

_____

_____

_____

_____

_____

_____

Lesson **31** Rental Advertisements

Exercise 1   Read this ad and then answer the questions.

> Manhattan-E. 64 St. 1 Br. 1 bath- a/c, near shopg elev. walk RR, $1025/mo. garage rent. 555–7831 ev.

1. Where is the dwelling located? _____

_____

2. Is it in a walk-up or a building with an elevator? _____

_____

3. How many bedrooms does it have? _____

_____

4. How many bathrooms does it have? _____

_____

5. Is it near shopping? _____

_____

6. Is it near transportation? _____

_____

Is it near the train or bus? _____

How do you know? _____

7. How much is the rent? _____

_____

8. What can you do if you have a car? _____

_____

9. What must you do to find out more about this apartment? _____

_____

10. When can you call? _____

_____

Exercise 2   Read the dialogue.

Mr. Amar is talking to the superintendent of an apartment building.

Mr. Amar: I understand that you have an apartment for rent.

Super: Yes. It has three bedrooms, a living room, a kitchen, and a bathroom. It's on the fourth floor, and there are no elevators.

Mr. Amar: Is there air conditioning?

Super: There is air conditioning in the bedrooms but not in the kitchen or the living room.

Mr. Amar: Is the stove electric or gas?

Super: It's a gas stove.

Mr. Amar: Good. That way you can't burn yourself so easily.

Super: I'll show you the apartment. If you like it, you can sign a three-year lease for $530 a month rent.

Mr. Amar: I'll take a look, but then I must bring my wife and kids. I can't sign until they see the place, too.

Super: Come between 6:00 and 8:00 P.M. I'll be here then.

Mr. Amar: Thanks. We'll be back tomorrow.

Super: Fine. Now follow me and I'll show you the apartment.

Exercise 3   Make up five questions about the dialogue.

1. _____

2. _____

3. _____

4. _____

5. _____

Exercise 4   Now answer the questions you made up.

1. _____

2. _____

3. _____

4. _____

5. _____

Lesson **32** Review of Rooms and Furnishings

Exercise 1   Write the correct word above each picture.

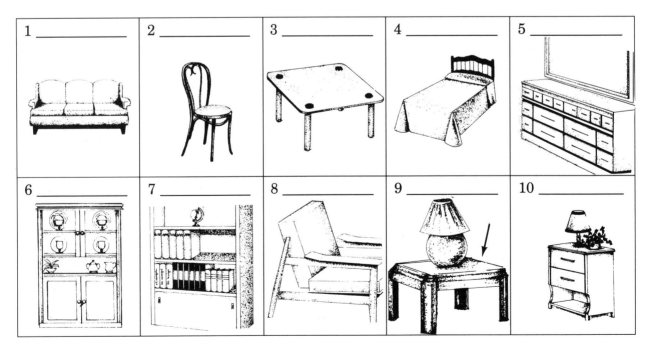

Exercise 2   Unscramble the words to find the names of household items. Then match the words to the pictures. Write the letter of the correct picture next to each word.

____ 1. p a l m _____
____ 2. s k i n _____
____ 3. v o t e s _____
____ 4. treeirrfgaor _____
____ 5. h a t b u t b _____
____ 6. i l e t t o _____
____ 7. u r g _____
____ 8. s a u t i c r n _____
____ 9. hrats nac _____
____ 10. neiimdce banciet _____

____ 11. s t i u c r p e _____
____ 12. t o p _____
____ 13. n a p _____
____ 14. s l o w e t _____
____ 15. v e l s a i r r e w _____
____ 16. m u a u c v _____
____ 17. w i l l o p _____
____ 18. b r e n d l e _____
____ 19. l n e b a k t _____
____ 20. m a r e p h _____

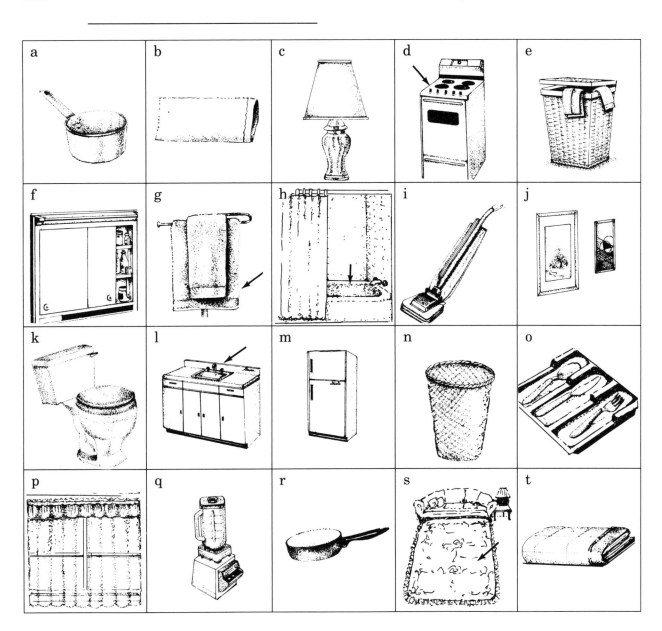

Exercise 3   Complete the sentences.

1. We keep food cold in a _____ .

2. Two or three people can sit on a _____ .

3. We wash dishes in the _____ or _____ .

4. Bathroom floors and walls are often made of _____ .

5. We put dirty clothes in a _____ .

Exercise 4   Answer these questions in complete sentences.

1. What are two things we can find in every room in a home? _____

    _____

2. What do we do in a bathtub? _____

    _____

3. What do we find in a bedroom? _____

    _____

4. Where do we wash our faces? _____

    _____

5. Where do we keep our clean clothing? _____

    _____

Exercise 5   Match the items with their locations.

A	B
____ 1. rug	a. kitchen cabinets
____ 2. blankets, sheets, and pillowcases	b. bookcase
____ 3. dishes	c. floor
____ 4. vacuum cleaner	d. bathroom walls and floors
____ 5. table and chairs	e. bed
____ 6. books	f. dresser
____ 7. venetian blinds	g. broom closet
____ 8. tile	h. windows
____ 9. clothes	i. kitchen or dining room

Exercise 6   Identify each object and name the room in which you can find it.

1. This is a _____ .

   It is in the _____ .

2. This is a _____ .

   It is in the _____ .

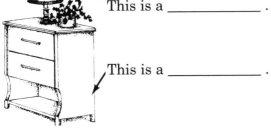

3. 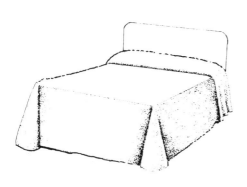 This is a _____ .

   This is a _____ .

   They are in the _____ .

4. This is an _____ .

   It is in the _____ .

5. This is a _____ .

   It is in the _____ .

6. This is a _____ .

   It is in the _____ .

7. This is a _____ .

It is in the _____ .

8. This is a _____ .

It is in the _____ .

9. This is a _____ .

It is in the _____ .

10. This is a _____ .

It is in the _____ .

Exercise 7   Identify these parts of a house or an apartment. Write the correct words above the pictures.

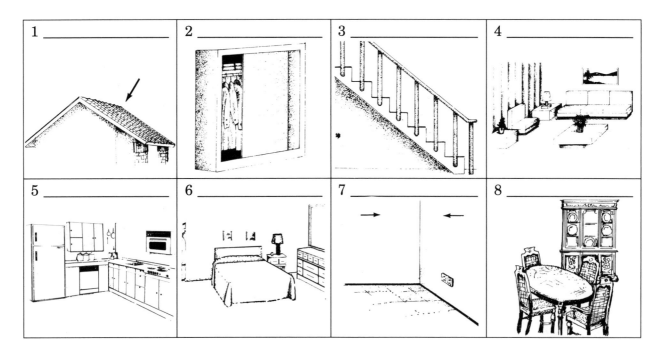

1 _____

2 _____

3 _____

4 _____

5 _____

6 _____

7 _____

8 _____

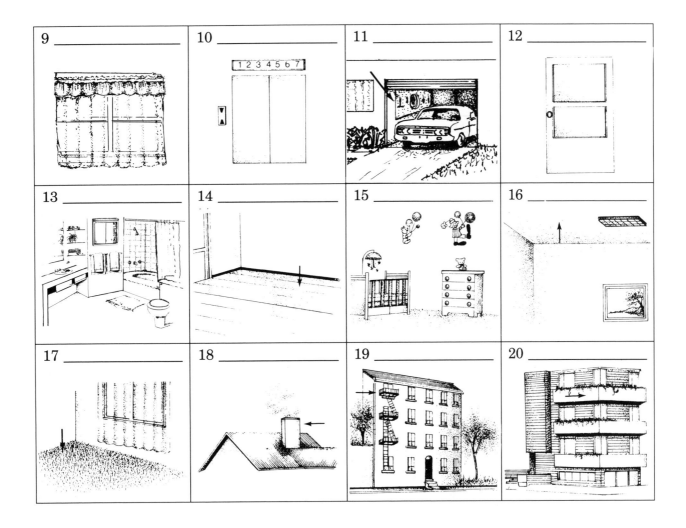

9 ———	10 ———	11 ———	12 ———
13 ———	14 ———	15 ———	16 ———
17 ———	18 ———	19 ———	20 ———

Exercise 8   Unscramble the words at the left. Write one letter in each box at the right. Then unscramble the letters in the circles to spell out the mystery words.

1. r s e d s e r

2. t h e s e

3. l e a t k b n

Mystery Word: ___ ___ ___

1. k o k o

2. v o t e s

3. fearrteroigr

4. n e b a i t c s

Mystery Word: ___ ___ ___ ___

Exercise 9   Find and circle the hidden words. Look across, down, diagonally, forward, and backward. Then find the four letters you do not use. Unscramble them to find the name of part of a house. Write the mystery word below the puzzle.

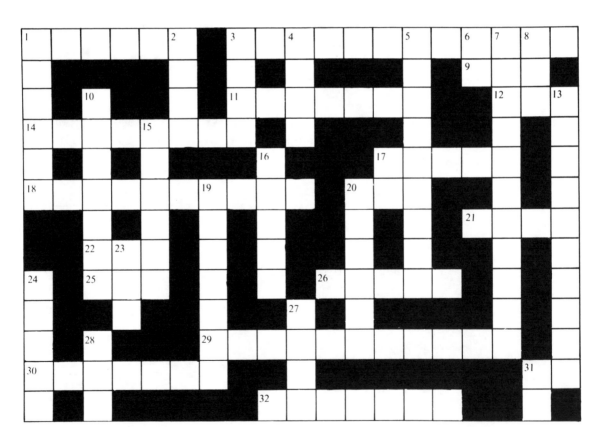

B	H	O	S	C	F	L	O	O	R
R	T	M	I	H	L	F	R	V	U
E	O	A	L	A	V	O	O	E	G
A	L	T	V	I	A	S	S	N	S
K	C	E	E	R	C	T	P	E	S
F	E	P	R	B	U	A	M	P	T
R	L	R	W	R	U	I	A	O	O
O	B	A	A	O	M	R	L	T	V
N	A	C	R	O	S	I	N	K	E
T	T	N	E	M	T	R	A	P	A

apartment	oven
breakfront	pot
broom	rugs
carpet	silverware
chair	sink
closet	stair
floor	stove
lamp	tablecloth
mat	vacuum

Mystery Word: __ __ __ __

Exercise 10   Complete the crossword puzzle.

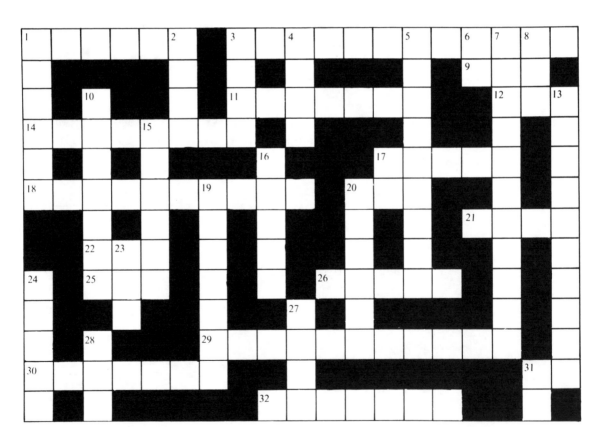

Across

1 In the bathtub we can take a bath or a _____ .

3 Food stays cold in the _____ .

9 My father is a _____ .

Everyday English, Book Two

11 Another word for trash is _____ .

12 I sleep in my _____ .

14 Items of furniture with drawers for storing clothes are called _____ .

17 We eat lunch at the kitchen _____ .

18 A knife, fork, and spoon are _____ .

20 We cook the food in a big _____ .

21 Here is the architect's _____ for our new house.

22 Mom is _____ in the living room. She's in the bedroom.

25 I have a _____ stove, not an electric one.

26 Drink from this _____ .

29 _____ cover the pillows.

30 We clean carpets with _____ .

31 I _____ in the kitchen.

32 The bed is in the _____ .

Down

1 Venetian blinds or _____ can keep out sunlight.

2 We put on a bath_____ after we take a bath.

3 Small carpets are _____ .

4 A knife, a spoon, and a _____ are silverware

5 Walk-ups have no _____ .

6 I _____ living in an apartment now.

7 _____ cover tables.

8 My apartment has _____ bedroom.

10 The lights are in the _____ .

13 The _____ _____ is for eating and entertaining.

15 _____ and blankets go on the bed.

17 Come _____ my house.

16 I sweep the floor with a _____ .

19 Apartment buildings with stairs only are called _____ .

20 I put my head on the _____ .

23 I eat _____meal in a bowl for breakfast.

24 Be careful! The _____ is hot.

27 The walls are painted _____ .

28 There are _____ cubes in the freezer.

31 Is someone _____ the door?

Exercise 11   Add the suggested letters to make new words. You may need to rearrange the letters in the old words to make the new ones.

1. t h e s e + s = _____

2. r a i n + d = _____

3. l o c k + c = _____

4. m a p + l = _____

5. p a n t s + l = _____

6. l a w + l = _____

7. r o o f + l = _____

8. l a t e + b = _____

9. i n k + s = _____

10. c l o s e + t = _____

Unit
7 Careers

Lesson 33 Some Occupations

Exercise 1   Make a list of occupations you already know something about. Add to the list as your class discusses other careers.

_____   _____

_____   _____

_____   _____

_____   _____

_____   _____

_____   _____

_____   _____

_____   _____

_____   _____

Exercise 2   Study these sentences with your teacher.

1. She examines and treats patients. She's a doctor.
2. She works in a hospital. She's a nurse.
3. He repairs cars. He's a mechanic.
4. He delivers our letters and packages. He's a mail carrier.
5. She flies a plane. She's a pilot.
6. He presides over a court of law. He's a judge.
7. She designs buildings. She's an architect.
8. He designs bridges and tunnels. He's an engineer.
9. She represents a client in court. She's a lawyer.
10. He fixes pipes. He's a plumber.

Exercise 3   Answer these questions in complete sentences.

1. What does a lawyer do? _____

    _____

2. What does a pilot do? _____

    _____

3. What does a mechanic do?_____

    _____

4. What does a doctor do? _____

    _____

5. What does an architect do? _____

    _____

Exercise 4   Write **T** if a sentence is true. Write **F** if it is false.

1. A nurse works in a hospital.   _____

2. A mail carrier delivers babies.   _____

3. An engineer drives a bus.   _____

4. A plumber fixes pipes.   _____

5. A judge presides over a court of law.   _____

Exercise 5   Study these sentences with your teacher.

1. She paints. She's an artist.
2. He writes books. He's an author.
3. She's the head of a school. She's a principal.
4. He sells meat. He's a butcher.
5. She bakes bread. She's a baker.
6. He fixes lights. He's an electrician.
7. She types letters. She's a secretary.
8. He makes and alters clothes. He's a tailor.
9. He serves food in a restaurant. He's a waiter.
10. She serves food in a restaurant. She's a waitress.

Exercise 6   Match the words in column A with the words in column B to make sentences.

A	B
____ 1. A waiter	a. bakes bread.
____ 2. A butcher	b. paints.
____ 3. A principal	c. serves food.
____ 4. A baker	d. sells meat.
____ 5. A tailor	e. types.
____ 6. An electrician	f. writes books.
____ 7. A secretary	g. serves food.
____ 8. An artist	h. fixes lights.
____ 9. An author	i. is in charge of a school.
____ 10. A waitress	j. makes clothes.

Exercise 7   Complete the names of these occupations. Look at the words below if you need help.

plumber	principal	doctor	baker	artist
mechanic	waitress	pilot	butcher	judge

1. __ __ k e __
2. __ __ __ t r __ __ __
3. __ u t __ __ __ __
4. __ __ __ __ c i __ __ __
5. __ __ t i __ __

6. __ __ c t __ __
7. __ i l __ __
8. __ __ __ m b __ __
9. __ __ d g __
10. __ __ c h __ __ __ __

Lesson 34 What Workers Do on the Job

Exercise 1   Study these sentences with your teacher.

1. He takes pictures. He's a photographer.
2. He fights crime. He's a police officer.
3. She makes movies. She's a director.
4. She plays an instrument. She's a musician.

5. He helps people learn. He's a teacher.

6. She takes care of people's teeth. She's a dentist.

7. She takes your money in a store. She's a cashier.

8. He cuts people's hair. He's a hair stylist.

9. She takes away our trash. She's a garbage collector.

10. He takes care of the house and the children. He's a homemaker.

Exercise 2   Identify the person by reading about the occupation, or identify the occupation by reading about the person.

1. I fight crime.   I'm a _____ .

2. I fix people's teeth.   I'm a _____ .

3. I _____ .   I'm a garbage collector.

4. I _____ .   I'm a hair stylist.

5. I _____ .   I'm a teacher.

6. I make movies.   I'm a _____ .

7. I play an instrument.   I'm a _____ .

8. I _____ .   I'm a cashier.

9. I take care of the house.   I'm a _____ .

10. I _____ .   I'm a photographer.

Exercise 3   Study these sentences with your teacher.

1. He drives a tractor. He's a farmer.

2. She fixes meals in a restaurant. She's a chef.

3. He sells things. He's a salesperson.

4. She writes music. She's a composer.

5. He arranges vacations and other trips. He's a travel agent.

6. She makes wooden furniture. She's a carpenter.

7. He fills your doctor's prescription. He's a pharmacist.

8. She writes for a newspaper. She's a reporter.

9. He does your taxes. He's an accountant.

10. He's in the movies and on TV. He's an actor.

11. She's in the movies and on TV. She's an actress.

Exercise 4   Find and circle the hidden words. The clues below will tell you what words to look for. Look forward, across, down, diagonally, and backward. Then find the twelve letters you do not use. Unscramble them to spell out a mystery word. Write the mystery word below the puzzle.

D	L	R	I	R	B	T	C	R	E	S
A	O	A	C	F	A	R	M	E	R	E
R	A	C	T	O	R	E	E	E	E	C
C	D	E	T	E	B	D	C	N	S	R
H	E	R	K	O	E	S	H	I	O	E
I	R	A	I	N	R	R	A	G	P	T
T	B	S	T	N	A	O	N	N	M	A
E	P	I	L	O	T	T	I	E	O	R
C	S	J	O	B	S	C	C	L	C	Y
T	R	A	V	E	L	A	G	E	N	T
S	T	N	A	T	N	U	O	C	C	A

Clues

1. A _____ examines patients.

2. A _____ cuts men's hair.

3. A _____ writes music.

4. A _____ drives a tractor.

5. A _____ fixes teeth.

6. An _____ designs buildings.

7. A _____ can arrange your vacation.

8. _____ do your taxes.

9. _____ are in movies.

10. A _____ types.

11. A _____ makes bread and cakes.

12. A _____ flies planes.

13. A _____ fixes cars.

14. An _____ is a man who acts.

15. Someone who loads is a _____ .

16. Someone who races is a _____ .

17. An _____ builds bridges and tunnels.

18. People who are employed have _____ .

Mystery Word: __ __ __ __ __ __ __ __ __ __ __ __

Everyday English, Book Two

Exercise 5   Choose two careers you would like to have. Find some information about them and write a short paragraph about each one. Explain what you must do on the job, what education you need, and what training you require. Do you already have some knowledge or experience in this field? Why is this a good job to have? Why do you want this job?

_____

_____

_____

_____

_____

_____

_____

_____

Lesson **35** More Occupations

Exercise 1   Choose twenty-five occupations and write each one in a box on the Bingo card. Your teacher will then describe many occupations. If you hear about an occupaton that's on your Bingo card, cover that square with a small piece of paper. If you cover five boxes across, five down, or five diagonally, you say "Bingo!"

B	**I**	**N**	**G**	**O**

Exercise 2

Unscramble the names of these occupations. Then write a sentence describing each one.

Example: c r a t o   <u>actor</u> / <u>An actor stars in movies and television shows.</u>

1. r e o h a m k e m   _____ / _____

   _____

2. e h r t c a e   _____ / _____

   _____

3. m l r u p e b   _____ / _____

   _____

4. t a h o u r   _____ / _____

   _____

5. c r n l i p p i a   _____ / _____

   _____

6. w e r a y l   _____ / _____

   _____

7. c i o p l e   r f o f i c e   _____ / _____

   _____

8. r a e m f r   _____ / _____

   _____

9. n i s d t e t   _____ / _____

   _____

10. c a u t n c o n a t   _____ / _____

   _____

Exercise 3

Here are the names of more occupations. See how many of them you know something about. Talk about these jobs with your teacher, and then write a sentence about each one on a separate piece of paper.

1. firefighter   7. grocer
2. athlete   8. superintendent
3. truck driver   9. factory worker
4. crossing guard   10. bookkeeper
5. shoemaker   11. taxicab driver
6. zookeeper   12. bus driver

13. conductor	32. stockbroker
14. construction worker	33. computer analyst
15. real estate agent	34. fashion designer
16. clerk	35. bank teller
17. roofer	36. mayor
18. banker	37. editor
19. landlord / landlady	38. president
20. librarian	39. soldier
21. boxer	40. poet
22. flight attendant	41. singer
23. miner	42. dancer
24. navigator	43. umpire
25. researcher	44. coach
26. jeweler	45. maid
27. security guard	46. politician
28. producer	47. wrestler
29. manager	48. stenographer
30. mover	49. gardener
31. lifeguard	50. sailor

Lesson 36 Seeking Employment

Exercise 1   Study these sentences with your teacher.

1. When you have a **full-time** job, you work about forty hours a week.

2. When you have a **part-time** job, you usually work fewer than five days a week.

3. In a **job interview**, you are asked questions about yourself and your qualifications to see if you will be good for the job.

4. When you **cancel** an appointment, you say that you cannot come.

5. When you **postpone** an appointment, you put it off for another time.

6. A **résumé** is a written summary of your work, education, and other experiences that are related to the job you are seeking.

7. A **temporary job** is a job that will last only for a certain period of time (days, weeks, or months).

8. A **permanent job** is a job that is ongoing; the position is expected to exist for many years.

9. An **employment agency** is an organization that helps people find work.

Exercise 2   Match the words with their definitions.

	A		**B**
____	1. temporary job	a.	working from 8:00 A.M. to 5:00 P.M. Monday through Friday
____	2. part-time job	b.	say you cannot come
____	3. cancel	c.	meeting of an employer and a possible employee
____	4. résumé	d.	organization that helps you find work
____	5. permanent job	e.	want-ad section of a newspaper
____	6. postpone	f.	lasts for years
____	7. interview	g.	working from 9:00 A.M. to 12:30 P.M. Monday through Friday
____	8. employment agency	h.	a written summary of your work and educational experiences
____	9. full-time job	i.	put off
____	10. classified ads	j.	lasts only a certain period of time

Exercise 3   Complete this résumé about yourself.

Name _____

Address _____

City _____ State _____ Zip Code _____

Telephone _____

Educational Background
(Begin with the institution most recently attended.)

School	**Dates of Attendance**	**Degree**
_____	_____	_____
_____	_____	_____
_____	_____	_____
_____	_____	_____
_____	_____	_____

Job Experience
(Begin with the most recent position.)

Establishment	Dates of Employment	Position	Reason for Leaving
_____	_____	_____	_____
_____	_____	_____	_____
_____	_____	_____	_____
_____	_____	_____	_____
_____	_____	_____	_____

Languages spoken fluently: _____

_____

Honors and Achievements

_____

_____

_____

_____

Activities (hobbies, organizations)

_____

_____

_____

_____

References

Name	Address	Position
_____	_____	_____
_____	_____	_____
_____	_____	_____
_____	_____	_____

Exercise 4   Write **T** if a sentence is true. Write **F** if it is false.

1. A résumé is a canceled interview.   _____

2. To postpone something is to put it off for
   another day.   _____

3. A temporary job must be part time.   _____

4. Working half a day is a full-time job.   _____

5. An employment agency helps you look for a job.   _____

Exercise 5   Read these ads and answer the questions about them.

a.
> SP / ENG. Sec'y for busy ad agency. Must
> have steno 100+ and / or dictaphone exp. Pt.
> time poss. Send resume. Job Agency 13 E. 23
> St. N.Y. 10018

1. What kind of job is this?_____

2. How much does it pay? _____

3. Must you know stenography? _____

4. What does *steno 100+* mean? _____

5. What is *exp.*? _____

6. Must you send a résumé?_____

7. What is the name of the agency? _____

8. What is the agency's address? _____

9. Can you call about the job? _____

10. How many languages must you know?_____

11. Which languages must you know?_____

b.
> WAITERS m / f, full & p / t needed N.Y. exec.
> din. rm. facility. Min. 1 yr exp. req'd. For app't
> call Joe Smith Mon.–Fri. betw 8–11 A.M. at
> 555–5922.

1. How much does this job pay? _____

2. Is it full time or part time? _____

3. What kind of job is it? _____

4. Where will you work? _____

5. What does *min.* mean? _____

6. What does *req'd* mean? _____

7. Should you write or call about the job? _____

8. When should you call? _____

9. Is the job for men only? _____

10. What does *app't* mean? _____

11. Who should you call? _____

Exercise 6   Write the correct word above each picture.

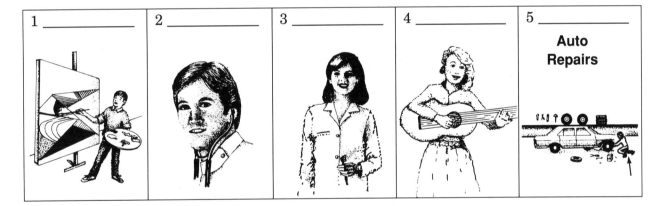

Lesson 37 Job Interviews

Exercise 1   Study this dialogue with your teacher.

Helena is interviewing at an employment agency. Let's see what happens.

Ms. Meza: Come in, please, and take a seat. What can I do for you?

Helena: I'd like a part-time job, five afternoons a week.

Ms. Meza: Is this a temporary or a permanent job you're looking for?

Helena: It's a permanent job. I go to school in the mornings, and I
want to work in the afternoons.

Ms. Meza:	What are you interested in doing?
Helena:	I can do a little bit of everything. I worked in an office last summer, and I taught children in an after-school center during the winter. Here is my résumé.
Ms. Meza:	That looks very good. Let's see. I have openings for a dental receptionist and a typist. I'll set up an interview for you at both places. Please call me if you want to postpone or cancel an interview, or if you get one of the jobs. I'll keep your résumé on file. Take another copy with you to each job interview. Good luck to you.
Helena:	Thank you. Good-bye.
Ms. Meza:	Good-bye.

Exercise 2   Answer these questions in complete sentences.

1. What is an employment agency? _____

_____

2. What kind of job does Helena want?_____

_____

3. What can Helena do? _____

_____

4. Where did she work last summer? _____

_____

5. Where did she work last winter?_____

_____

6. For what jobs does Ms. Meza have openings? _____

_____

7. What must Helena do if she wants to cancel or postpone an interview?

_____

8. What must Helena take to her interviews? _____

_____

9. Have you ever had a job? _____

_____

If so, where did you work? _____

_____

10. Do you want to work next summer? _____

_____

If so, what would you like to do? _____

_____

Lesson 38 Review of Careers

Exercise 1 Complete the sentences.

1. A _____ brings us mail.

2. A _____ fights crime.

3. A _____ bakes cakes.

4. A _____ sells meat.

5. A _____ makes and alters clothes.

6. A _____ helps people learn.

7. A _____ can arrange your vacation.

8. A _____ plays an instrument.

9. A _____ makes wooden furniture.

10. A _____ cuts hair.

Exercise 2 Answer these questions in complete sentences.

1. What does a dentist do? _____

2. What does a pilot do? _____

3. What does a mechanic do? _____

4. What does a plumber do? _____

5. What does a cashier do?_____

6. What does a nurse do? _____

7. What does an author do? _____

8. What does a principal do? _____

9. What does a judge do? _____

10. What does an architect do? _____

Exercise 3   Match these people with their jobs.

A	B
____ 1. dentist	a. works with students
____ 2. composer	b. takes care of people's teeth
____ 3. secretary	c. fixes lights
____ 4. teacher	d. grows fruits, vegetables, and grains
____ 5. electrician	e. takes away trash
____ 6. plumber	f. takes your money
____ 7. cashier	g. speak for their clients
____ 8. farmer	h. fixes pipes
____ 9. garbage collector	i. writes music
____ 10. lawyers	j. types

Exercise 4   Write the meanings of these words.

1. full time _____

2. postpone _____

3. interview _____

4. part time _____

5. cancel _____

Exercise 5   Answer these questions in complete sentences.

    1. What is a temporary job? _____

    _____

    2. What is a résumé? _____

    _____

    3. What is a permanent job? _____

    _____

    4. Who needs to have a résumé? _____

    _____

Exercise 6   Complete the names of these occupations. Then read the circled letters to find the mystery career.

    1. Ⓞ __ L O __

    2. Ⓞ __ W Y __ __

    3. M Ⓞ __ __ C I __ __

    4. Ⓞ __ C H __ __ __ C

    5. Ⓞ U __ __ __ E R

    6. T Ⓞ __ C H __ __

    7. A Ⓞ __ __ __ __ E C T

    Mystery Career: P_ __ __ __ __ __ __

Exercise 7   Write the name of an occupation for each letter in the word nurse. The letter can be at the beginning, in the middle, or at the end of your word. For example, the *N* can be part of the word ba*n*ker, politicia*n*, or *n*avigator.

    _____ N _____

    _____ U _____

    _____ R _____

    _____ S _____

    _____ E _____

Exercise 8   Complete the crossword puzzle.

Across

1 If you want to work, there are many _____ to choose from.

3 An _____ designs houses.

7 A doctor treats you when you are _____ .

8 A _____ works with students.

9 _____ fly planes.

12 Mail carrier _____ a synonym for <u>postal</u> <u>worker</u>.

13 A _____ types letters.

16 Some people work _____ days a week.

17 You can be either a doctor _____ a lawyer.

19 A dancer is full _____ energy.

20 Women who are hired to clean houses or other buildings are _____ .

22 A _____ fixes cars.

25 A musician reads musical _____ .

27 A job that lasts from 9:00 A.M. to 1:00 P.M. is a _____ - _____ job.

28 Look in the _____ for a job.

30 _____ _____ can arrange your vacations.

31 Cashiers _____ your money in the supermarket.

Down

1 A _____ presides over a courtroom.

2 A _____ sells meat.

3 A doctor tries to cure _____ and pains.

4 Another word for <u>automobile</u> is _____ .

5 Look in the _____ section of the newspaper for want ads.

6 A _____ speaks for his clients.

7 An interview _____ a meeting between two or more people.

10 You can buy a _____ in a toy store.

11 A painter is an _____ .

14 An _____ designs roads and bridges.

15 You need two _____ for a soccer game.

16 This father and _____ are in business together.

18 A cashier gives you _____ when you pay too much money.

19 Get to work _____ time.

21 _____ you want to be a police officer?

23 A truck driver drives a _____ .

24 Which _____ do you want to buy?

26 An artist paints on an _____ .

27 A _____ writes poems.

29 Painting and sculpture are two types of _____ .